Hemingway's Spanish ༄ ༄ ༄
Tragedy ༄ ༄

by LAWRENCE R. BROER

THE UNIVERSITY OF ALABAMA PRESS
University, Alabama

THIS STUDY IS DEDICATED TO CÉSAR LUIS RIVERA, PROFES-
SOR OF SPANISH AT ST. PETERSBURG JUNIOR COLLEGE, WHO
NOT ONLY HELPED COMPILE A BIBLIOGRAPHY ON THE SPAN-
ISH CHARACTER, BUT ALSO GAVE INVALUABLE HELP IN MAT-
TERS OF TRANSLATION. ALSO A DEBT OF GRATITUDE GOES
OUT TO CARMEN AVILA AND KRISTINE SHIELDS, WHO
HELPED IN MORE WAYS THAN ONE. FINAL THANKS ARE DUE
DR. RICHARD CARPENTER AND DR. FRANK BALDANZA,
WHOSE COGENT CRITICISMS BOTH INSPIRED AND GAVE
MEANINGFUL DIRECTION TO MUCH OF THE WRITING OF THIS
BOOK.

The various passages from the works of Ernest Hemingway
included in this book are protected by copyright and have been
quoted with the permission of Charles Scribner's Sons.

Contents

Abbreviations for Hemingway's Works

ART   *Across The River And Into The Trees.* New York: Charles Scribner's Sons, 1950.

B-L   *By-Line: Ernest Hemingway.* New York: Bantam Books, 1967.

DA   *Death In The Afternoon.* New York: Charles Scribner's Sons, 1932.

DS   *The Dangerous Summer.* Serialized in *Life* magazine, September 5, 12, 19, 1960.

FA   *A Farewell To Arms.* New York: Charles Scribner's Sons, 1929.

FC   *The Fifth Column And Four Unpublished Stories Of The Spanish Civil War.* New York: Bantam Books, 1969.

FWBT   *For Whom The Bell Tolls.* New York: Charles Scribner's Sons, 1940.

GHA   *Green Hills Of Africa.* New York: Doubleday & Co., 1954.

HHN   *To Have And Have Not.* New York: Charles Scribner's Sons, 1937.

IOT   *In Our Time.* New York: Charles Scribner's Sons, 1925.

MF   *A Moveable Feast.* New York: Charles Scribner's Sons, 1964.

OMS   *The Old Man And The Sea.* New York: Charles Scribner's Sons, 1952.

SR   *The Sun Also Rises.* New York: Charles Scribner's Sons, 1926.

SS   *The Short Stories Of Ernest Hemingway.* New York: Charles Scribner's Sons, 1927.

Introduction

Carlos Baker has written, "For years before he won the Nobel Prize in literature at the age of fifty-five, Ernest Hemingway had been a citizen of the world." Baker was referring to the fact that Hemingway's gargantuan passion for travel and adventure had carried him on a spiritual expedition into every country of western and eastern Europe, the Middle East, Asia and Australia, and into the northern and southern parts of America and Africa. So, in one sense, Hemingway had indeed earned the right to be called "world citizen."

Sean O'Faolain said it was probably Hemingway's spirit of gallantry which made him rove the world in search of the flame of spirit in men and beasts.[1] Whatever his motives, his peripatetic nature—his penchant for searching out new dangers in remote corners of the world—led the Nobel award spokesman to say, upon issuing the author his 1954 Nobel Prize, "We might as well give it to him now before he kills himself in some adventure."[2]

There were, of course, many countries of which Hemingway was especially fond. He often spoke of his infatuation with France, whose capital he saw as a continual excitation of the senses. He spoke, too, with special affection for Italy. And Africa represented to him freedom, wildness, and adventure. Yet one country Hemingway loved above all others, a country whose capital was "the best city in the world," a country that fed his soul and gave sustenance to his most intimate longings: his "beloved Spain."

Van Wyck Brooks once said about the spiritual disinheritance of American writers, "When we leave our country, we are apt to leave our roots behind us, and we fail to develop roots in any other country." This was clearly not the case with Hemingway, who might have answered Brooks in this way: "Where a man feels

v

at home, outside of where he's born, is where he's meant to go" (*GHA*, 191). Because Hemingway could not identify with the land of his birth, its social patterns or modes of existence, he had to travel 3,000 miles to a country remote from his own in time and space, but one whose emotional distance could be bridged with no trouble at all.

Postwar disillusionment had driven Hemingway into exile in Paris, but he chose Spain as his spiritual home. This still ancient country and the particular temperamental bent of its people struck a dramatically responsive chord in Hemingway's nature. Here was a land and a people, he marveled, still enticingly primitive in character, that had remained "unspoiled" amid the overcrowding and modernization of twentieth-century life.

Though the author's interest in Spain centered on the bullfight, his knowledge of Spain drew upon a wealth of experience in that country, and it took many stories and novels and a play to express all that it meant to him as man and artist. He traveled in Spain periodically for over forty years, getting to know the country from the inside—its people and their particular customs and sensibilities. He came to speak the Spanish language almost as a native, and genuine Spanish swear words and idioms are copiously scattered all over the pages of his books, along with Spanish gestures in intonation and manner. Philip Young has noted that "The conversation of his heroes has always a distinctly Spanish flavor—rigid, tense, verging on bravado," [3] and Arturo Baera commented on Hemingway's "astonishingly real Spanish conversation" and the "primitive realism and capacity to catch every emotion that was felt by the people as a whole." [4]

But Hemingway's interest in the Spanish people and their way of life is scarcely as simple or superficial as this. The Spanish element in Hemingway's fiction is never mere backdrop—a setting for new adventures—often it is the very lifeblood of the ideas and artistic methods he employs. He especially identified himself with the Spaniard's extraordinary interest in violence and death, which corresponded to his own and which subsequently helped him to isolate and crystalize the fundamental spiritual attitude at the core of his life and work. Thus, it was mainly in terms of the Spanish bullfight that Hemingway attempted to define his highest aspirations as man and artist. In the last act of the *corrida*—the moment of truth—he found a metaphor, or an objective correlative, for the heart of his work. And in the image of the matador, he found a symbol of the best a man can be in a violent and irrational world—a model of manhood and integrity after which he would pattern his major fictional heroes.

It is the purpose of this work, then, to 1) investigate the reasons for Hemingway's extensive interest in the Spanish people and their way of life, 2) identify those aspects of the Spanish world that appear to have directly influenced the author's art, and 3) explain the effects of these on his interpretation of the world around him and on his rendering of character. This final objective constitutes the core of this study; that is, Hemingway's attachment to Spanish thinking resulted in a marked change in the mental disposition and behavioral patterns of his heroes.

Whereas Hemingway's early heroes, those least affected by the author's Spanish enthusiasms, evince a sense of vulnerability and helplessness in the face of life's uncertainties, his later heroes—those conceived after the author's emotional and artistic commitment to what he came to view as the Spaniard's *particularismo*—are distinctly aggressive and bellicose in nature. These later heroes seem to derive unmistakably from Hemingway's sympathetic portraits of Pedro Romero, Juan Belmonte, and Manuel García Maera—those figures whom Hemingway apotheosizes in *The Sun Also Rises* and in his Spanish manifesto, *Death in the Afternoon*. These, Hemingway felt, were men worth emulating—men in the throes of perpetual conflict, who nevertheless were erect and proud looking, possessing a seemingly indomitable spirit and a sardonic carelessness.

Against the confusion and helplessness of Hemingway's protagonists conceived before 1932, these Spaniards who serve as models for Hemingway's later heroes live in accordance with a strict moral code that places a premium on stoical courage and perseverance and fosters an attitude of active rebellion in the face of inevitable defeat. These men are all faced with the same problems of fear, violence, and death that produce a state of emotional paralysis in the author's earlier characters, but the disdainful and recklessly aggressive manner in which they try to meet them designates, from their creator's standpoint, their moral superiority.

As a final introduction to this study, I wish to acknowledge a special indebtedness to Professor Carlos Baker for the invaluable information he has supplied on Hemingway's comings and goings in Spain in *Ernest Hemingway: A Life Story*. When I first wrote my introductory chapter, which examines Hemingway's experience as a lover of Spain and *aficionado* of the bullring, I found that accounts of his life in Spain and of his personal knowledge of Spanish culture were almost impossible to come by. But Professor Baker has shown us how extensively Hemingway visited Spain, how he got inside her soul, lived her life, and wove his experiences into the total fabric of his work.

Only two full-length studies of what Spain meant to Hemingway have come from the pens of Spaniards. In the preface to his book, *Hemingway Entre La Vida Y La Muerte* (published in 1968 by Ediciones Destino in Barcelona), Jose Luis Castillo-Puche acknowledges immediately the dearth of Spanish critical opinions about Spain's influence on Hemingway or what Hemingway may have meant to Spain. *Hemingway Y Los Sanfermines* (Pamplona, 1970), written by Jose Maria Iribarren, is the more limited of these two studies. It provides worthwhile corroboration of Hemingway's inside knowledge of the history and aesthetics of bullfighting, but is primarily a compilation of already existing accounts of Hemingway's visits to Pamplona over the course of his career. Bernard Oldsey, Professor of English at West Chester State College, who spent a year in Spain investigating Hemingway's life there, assures me that, despite the lack of commentary on the Hemingway-Spain affair, the Spaniards in general are aware from their reading of Hemingway that he did their country great services, not simply from the viewpoint of the civil war, but as a kind of patron, "an advertiser of great power and persuasion." Similar testimony has been given by the young Spanish-American writer and *Taurine* (one respected for having special knowledge of or insight into the aesthetics of bullfighting) Edward Perez. An annual follower of the bullfight circuit in Spain, Perez remarks that Hemingway's influence is particularly pervasive in Pamplona during the fiesta of San Fermín. He was surprised to find that the major bookstore in Pamplona promoted Hemingway as much as bullfighting itself, its display window serving as a veritable altar to the author's memory. Perez has noted that an additional indorsement by Spaniards of Hemingway's expert knowledge of Spanish culture comes in the form of an anthology of critical writings, personal essays, and short stories, entitled *Los Toros: Bullfighting*. The anthology is an exhaustive attempt to portray bullfighting in all its myriad facets, from multiple points of view. It conveys its origin, its history, its aesthetics, its major achievements and personalities, even memorable bulls. Not only are several central articles devoted to Hemingway's relationship to Spain and the bullfight, but it includes his short story "Capital of the World."

Jose Luis Castillo-Puche writes that Hemingway was the first modern writer to emphasize Spain as a subject and thus views his own work as the first cornerstone in "the monument of Spanish criticism on Hemingway that must come about in the future." [5] "Spain owes Ernest Hemingway a testimonial and sincere book," Castillo-Puche remarks, one that would serve in Spain as a tribute to its "most thorough and enthusiastic chronicler of modern times." He comments that Spain's debt to Hemingway is all the greater because the author did not make facile concessions to the tourist's view of Spain—did not treat only the beauty of the countryside and the surface manners of Spanish culture—but captured in his stories and his novels "a style of expression" and "an exceptional ethic" that bespeak an intimate knowledge of the Spanish spirit.[6] Castillo-Puche's friendship with Hemingway began in 1954, and they remained close friends until Hemingway died in 1961. Hemingway had just come back to Spain for the first time since the Spanish civil war. Castillo-Puche's first important novel had been brought to his attention *(Con La Muerte Al Hombro,* or *With Death At One's Shoulder),* and he touted it as the best, the most realistic novel he knew of by a living Spanish writer. A few years later he heaped similar praise on the doctor-novelist Pío Baroja y Nessi, telling him that he ought to have won the Nobel Prize. But Castillo-Puche claimed to be one of Hemingway's few carefully chosen confidants and said that it was the subject of his novel that cemented his relationship with the author. he explains that the character in his novel lives obsessed with the imminence of his own death—that death itself might very well be called the protagonist. This attracted and profoundly affected Hemingway, the writer observes. "It wasn't that Ernest carried death at his own shoulder, but that he carried it inside in the form of a bleeding wound. Only this obsession with death, almost mystical, can explain to us his fixation with the bullfight."[7]

For the most part, Castillo-Puche's study is a purely personal account of the author's friendship with Hemingway, filled with nostalgic memories of their travels and walks together through the streets of Madrid and other favorite Spanish towns. But at times he provides valuable insights into what he calls the intense drama that Hemingway's tortured spirit lived in Spain and, in particular, into those peculiarly Spanish aspects of his psyche that brought him into temperamental accord with the matador and with the spirit of the bullfight. Iribarren's *Hemingway Y Los Sanfermines* also contains useful personal reminiscences. Juanito Quintana, the fictional Montoya of *The Sun Also Rises*, introduced Iribarren to Hemingway in 1953, and they remained intimate friends until Hemingway's death. In addition to conveying Iribarren's wonder over and admiration for Hemingway's knowledge of bullfighting, his book emphasizes the intense personal pride that Hemingway took in his reputation as *aficionado*. "I realized that Hemingway knew of and had studied much of bullfighters," he says. "He always gave specifics to clarify and he knew the virtues and defects of each of the bullfighters."[8] He was equally impressed with Hemingway's recall of older matadors. Iribarren had remarked to Hemingway upon the greatness of the matador Joselito, noting the irony of his having been killed by a small bull. Hemingway responded, "He was a small bull, but he was a five year old bull." "That's true," Iribarren said. "But how come you know the bull that killed

Joselito was five years old?" "Oh, I know very much about the bulls," Hemingway followed, laughing at his boastfulness. "I believe it," Iribarren concluded. The author then observes: "He became very contented with my praise of him." [9] From time to time, I shall also illustrate certain affinities the author shared with the Spanish character and Spanish thinking by drawing from the works of Ortega y Gasset, Angel Ganivet, and Miguel de Unamuno. The last of these major surgeons of the Spanish personality, perhaps the greatest Spanish literary figure of the twentieth century, was one of three Spaniards who Hemingway said should have won the Nobel Prize in 1956.

Mary Hemingway and the mayor of Pamplona beside the monument dedicated to Hemingway in 1968.

1 / Traveler in Spain: An Overview

FROM THE time when Hemingway first visited the harbor town of Vigo, Spain, in December of 1921 until he left the Pamplona Festival for the last time in 1960, Spain was not only Hemingway's favorite vacation spot but a place for work and inspiration. He regularly found that he worked well there. He tells of a day in May, 1926—when snow had compelled cancellation of the bullfights in Madrid—during which he managed to complete three short stories between morning and evening.[1] He says in the introduction to his collected short stories, "Besides *The Fifth Column*, I wrote *The Killers, Today Is Friday, Ten Indians*, part of *The Sun Also Rises*, and the first third of *To Have And Have Not* in Madrid. It was always a good place for working."

As early as the age of twenty-two Hemingway began to indicate the impact the Spanish people would have on his life and work. His first look at Spain had actually come in 1919, on his homeward voyage from Italy to begin convalescence, when his boat touched briefly at Algeciras. But in 1921 at Vigo, he rejoiced in the primitive delights of its coast line and its market place, and began to sift his impressions of the bullfight as an integral part of Spanish culture even before he entered the bullrings of Spain.[2]

In 1923 he saw his first *novillada*—similar to a regular bullfight except that the bulls are often larger and more dangerous and are fought by bullfighters either too young or too old for a formal bullfight—at one of the outlying bullrings in Madrid, and its effect on him was so dramatic and so pervasive that it crowded everything else from his mind. In a personal interview, his wife Hadley re-

1

marked: "Ernest was completely fascinated with his first bullfight. We both were. I'm very proud, maybe ashamed to have liked it, loved it, from the beginning. Of course Ernest was there to explain it to me so that it made sense." His friends observed that almost immediately he began behaving like an initiate in a secret society. He could talk of nothing but the courage of the bulls and men and began making plans for a trip through Andalusia with a crew of matadors.[3] Already developing his characteristic scorn for those who did not share his enthusiasm for bullfights, he commented that foreigners were wrong in thinking that bullfights were brutal. Every *corrida*, he insisted, was "a great tragedy." Watching one was like having a ringside seat at a war.[4] If this final observation by the novice *aficionado* had a note of casualness and generality about it, perhaps it was because the author himself at this point had only instinctively glimpsed the immense emotional and artistic value of the parallel he had drawn.

Back in Paris, Hemingway immediately began dreaming of Spanish sunlight and of his first trip to the golden Basque country of Navarre, where early in July each year the fiesta, which lasted a week, attracted the best matadors in Spain. Hemingway spoke to his wife of the potentially salubrious prenatal influence of the bullfights on their baby and regretted that he had not brought with him a bull calf to practice veronicas with to fill up the time until he could return to Spain.[5]

Even though Hemingway seldom failed to attend the Fiesta of San Fermín in the years that followed, he later observed that his first visit had meant the most to him. Neither he nor Hadley had been prepared, Carlos Baker writes, for the perpetual excitement and drama that began that first sixth of July.

> The fiesta began with fireworks and continued through a noisy week of drinking and dancing, with religious processions and special Masses in the churches, and bullfights every afternoon. Each morning at dawn Ernest roused Hadley to watch the bulls come galloping down a mile and a half of cobblestoned streets to the pens in the Plaza de Toros. Ahead of the bulls ran all the young bucks of Pamplona, flirting with death and showing off to the crowds that were packed six deep along the route.

> Betweentimes came the riau-riau dancing, with men in blue shirts and red kerchiefs shuffling and singing through the streets and squares to the music of fifes and drums. The celebration reached its daily climax each afternoon at the bullfights. Five of the best matadors in Spain were gored in the first five days.[6]

So strong was the kinship Hemingway felt for two of the leading matadors at the fiesta, Manuel García and Nicanor Villalta, that he named his new son John Hadley Nicanor Hemingway in honor of Villalta and rejoiced in the fact that his son's nose made him resemble the King of Spain. He experienced a similar twinge of pride when a close friend remarked that with his dark hair and mustache, he appeared inconspicuous among his Spanish friends.

Before the month of July ended, Hemingway paid literary tribute to Villalta and Manuel García (called Maera) in a series of sketches from the world of the toreros that appeared in the vignettes of *in our time* [sic] (1924). And before the year was out, he even tried his hand at being a matador in Pamplona and wrote a long feature article about it in the *Toronto Star*—arguing that it was more tragedy than sport and writing of it as a symbol of life and death.[7] But the literary fruit of his love affair with "this most Christ-wonderful country in the world" had only begun to blossom. In the next two years his fascination with the patterned ritual of the bullfight and the artistry of the matador would occasion the memorable account of Garcia in "The Undefeated," the first of eight full-length short stories set in Spain, and then inspire his first major novel *The Sun Also Rises*. Hemingway called "The Undefeated" the "distillation of all he had learned about bullfighting in three visits to Spain." He viewed it as the best story he had ever written and noted in it the rich potential of a theme he had never tried before—that of a man who is destroyed but, because of the courageous fight he puts up against tremendous odds, not defeated. After *The Sun Also Rises*, the author continued in *Death In The Afternoon, For Whom The Bell Tolls*, and *The Dangerous Summer* to bear out the prophetic import of his first Pamplona adventure and of the initial inspiration of such men as Villalta and Maera.

During the crucial years of 1923-1926, when Hemingway was learning his craft and formulating personal theories of art, Spain was constantly in his thoughts. When he could not be there, he was longing for it, saving for it, dreaming of it, or vicariously enjoying it through contact with its painting or its language or its people. At home in Paris, he took solace in the piece of Spain that hung above his bed—a large, bright canvas called "The Farm" by a small, dark Spaniard named Joan Miró. Miró, he said, was the only painter who had ever been able to combine in one picture all that you felt about Spain when you were there and all that you felt when you were away and could not go there.[8] He dolefully observed to Gertrude Stein that despite his love for boxing, that sport looked pale beside the great sport of bullfighting, and said that he could hardly wait for the beginning of the next Fiesta of San Fermín in Pamplona. And playing tennis with Ezra Pound, he kept the image of Villalta and others alive by pretending that his racquet was a bullfighter's cape—dancing in front of trolley cars, executing correct and incorrect passes, and delightedly enraging the motorman.[9] His conversation took on a definite Spanish flavor as well. Waldo Pierce, a painter from Bangor, Maine, a large-spirited man whom Hemingway greatly admired, became, for instance, "Muy Caballero Mio"; and Ezra Pound, because of his boundless energy, merited comparison to "a fine Miura bull that no one ever shook a cape at without provoking a charge," and who "had fought all his fights with a very gay grimness. . . ." [10] In both instances, the bull and the bullfighter had become for Hemingway a simple and immediate measuring device for human conduct.

In comparison to the fiesta in 1923 and the one in 1925 that elicits the climactic passages of The Sun Also Rises, San Fermín in 1924 proved relatively calm. Hemingway wrote enthusiastically to Gertrude Stein that he was getting a lot of "dope" on bullfighting from the matadors who lived in the pension at 37, Calle San Jerónimo, and he took obvious joy in introducing such notables as Dos Passos and Bob McAlmon to the intricacies of the corrida. Probably the highlight of the fiesta came when the author, who "had been talking a good deal about courage" to Bob McAlmon and believed that "he must prove himself" during the free-for-all amateur bullfights held each morning, performed in the ring before 20,000 fans and then immediately reported the event to the *Toronto Star*.[11] But the fishing trip to the Basque village of Burguete in the mountains immediately after the fiesta proved equally memorable to him and deepened his love for Spain. The region was marked by ice-cold mountain streams and virgin beech forests which caused Hemingway to call it the wildest damn country in the Pyrenees. It was one of the few places left in Europe, he said, that had not been ruined by railroads and motorcars or that had not been shot to pieces.[12] The Spaniards, in fact, were the best people in the world—all of them "good guys." Spain was "the real old stuff."

In each year of the author's life, it seemed, the tide of events that began in Paris would climax in Spain. This was especially so in 1925, the year that Spain gave him the spiritual impetus he required to write his first major novel. Carlos Baker writes, "All through the winter in Schruns and the spring in Paris, Ernest had been dreaming of his third visit to the fiesta of San Fermín in Pamplona," [13] and dreaming in terms that suggested an increasingly primitive, almost bloodlust attraction to the elemental forces at work in the bullfight. Baker sums up the author's sentiments:

> Bulls were like rattlesnakes. They had been bred for speed and viciousness for 600 years, and reached the summit of their lives when they came tearing into the arena at ninety miles an hour. It was like prehistoric times to watch them chase a picador until they plucked him out of the saddle and gored him to death.[14]

But this year Hemingway had gathered together a small group of friends from the cafes of Montparnasse, the soon-to-be characters of *The Sun Also Rises*, whose idleness and irresponsibility cut heavily into his usual enjoyment of Pamplona. But for recompense he had the knowledge that these floaters of Montparnasse—Harold Loeb, Duff Twysden, and Pat Guthrie—were providing him with excellent literary capital, and the personal satisfaction that he was "tearing those bastards apart." [15]

Greater solace yet was to be found in the brilliant performances of a great new matador named Cayetano Ordóñez who was being hailed throughout Spain as the "Messiah who had come to save bullfighting." Hemingway immediately attached himself to the young torero, exalting in his suavity, the smoothness of his cape-work, and the dignified deliberation with which he moved in for the kill. Here was "purity of style itself," Hemingway praised,[16] and the courage to kill *"recibiendo,"* in the old manner of such eighteenth-century matadors as Pedro Romero. With the daily image of Ordóñez to inspire him, his novel began to take shape. It would embody what he had come to call "the fiesta concept of life," with Ordóñez as its hero and, by contrast, the relative unworthiness of his Paris friends as its major focus. Though the author would ultimately decide to set the opening of his novel in Paris, its original opening reflected its primary motivation. It began with his bullfighter hero as the center of interest, dressing for a fight in his hotel in the company of underlings and under the steady, worshipful gaze of an American named Jake Barnes.

By the end of his third consecutive fiesta, Hemingway had dra-matically established the intimate connection between his literary life and the life of Spain. If heaven was something that people enjoyed on earth rather than after death, then Spain was it. About this time he commented to Scott Fitzgerald that the bullfight had become the consuming passion of his life, to which everything else was subordinated. He said to Scott: "My idea of heaven is a big bullring where I have two permanent barrera seats." Even before *The Sun Also Rises* had been completed, he had begun to contemplate still another major work that would testify to the amazing extent to which Spain had permeated his consciousness. This would be a book, he said, that would do for the matadors and the animals what Doughty had done for the nomadic people of the Arabian deserts.[17] Another four years passed, however, before he turned back to what he called his major interest during this time and, in beginning work on his instructive treatise on the bullfight, achieved "the fulfillment of a five-year old dream." [18]

In the meantime, he threw himself into the Pamplona fiestas of 1926 and 1927 with as much gusto as ever, persuading close friends like Archibald MacLeish and others to share his passion for the bullfight, gathering materials and pictures for his book, and deepening his knowledge of those forces in the *corrida* that, in *Death in the Afternoon*, he would show to underlie the ruling philosophy of his life. By now even some of the author's non-Spanish stories had begun to take on a Spanish flavor. Along with another tribute to Maera in a piece called "Banal Story" published in a collection of stories entitled *Men Without Women* (1927), he included "The Killers" and a short one-act play called "Today is Friday." "The Killers" was written in Madrid, and the two original titles Hemingway is reported to have chosen for it, "The Matadors" and "Los Asesinos," reveal its Spanish orientation. His play is about three Roman soldiers drinking in a tavern in Jerusalem the evening after the crucifixion, but its dialogue, which centers on the courage and endurance of Christ's ordeal on the cross, might just as easily have concerned the heroic perseverance of Manuel Garcia in "The Undefeated" or Juan Belmonte in *The Sun Also Rises*. The image of one man alone, strong and self-reliant, attempting to persevere in the face of overwhelming odds, had, in fact, become the singularly most common ingredient in Hemingway's fiction at this time.

Hemingway missed the Pamplona fiesta in 1928. His second wife had undergone an agonizingly difficult childbirth, terminated by Caesarean section, and by the time that they were ready to travel the fiesta had passed them by. It was the first time since 1923 that he had missed the fiesta in Pamplona, and he grew deeply nostalgic. He would like to have been born there, he said, instead of only being able to get there in certain seasons. For a while he would have to enjoy Spain vicariously again through the Spanish architecture of his new home in Key West, Florida. Seeing it from across the street, Hemingway thought it resembled Joan Miró's "The Farm," which had kept him spiritually in touch with Spain during the early Paris days. By the summer of 1929, his longing for Spain was more intense than ever.

During the new season Hemingway engaged in the usual succession of bullfights, but the most important event of the summer was the appearance of a new bullfighting phenomenon named Sidney Franklin whom Hemingway would soon immortalize in a special appendix to *Death in the Afternoon*. Franklin's record during the summer had been impressive, and the Brooklyn *Daily Eagle* asked Hemingway to look him over. The author got to know him immediately, "A compensation for an otherwise unproductive summer," he said.[19] Franklin's valor was "cold, serene, and intelligent," and his artistry with the cape was beautiful to watch. From that time on Hemingway passed as much time with Franklin as possible, traveling through different parts of Spain together and exchanging views on bullfighting technique. Hemingway advised Franklin to kill with less sangfroid—to dramatize it more.[20] But ultimately he came to believe that Franklin's performance was "a marvel and a miracle." Hemingway seemed to take particular pride in the fact that Franklin liked him so much without any knowledge of his life as a writer. "I saw no reason to tell him that I had written any books," Hemingway said, but "someone finally told him that I was a novelist and he found it very hard to believe. This I took as a compliment." [21]

On his return to Paris, he wrote a bullfight article for *Fortune* magazine called "Bullfighting, Sport and Industry," which contained the seeds of the big book on the bullfight he had been long waiting to write. So determined now was he to get down in book form all the impressions he had gathered in nine years of intermittent contact with Spain and its people that he devoted almost the entire year of 1930 to its completion. And by the summer of 1931, it was nearly finished. He had finished eighteen chapters, including the compilation of a glossary of bullfight terms, and had even inserted events from the current bullfight season. By December, he had finished the "swell last chapter," a coda of 3,000 words that constituted his apologia for having concentrated on the bullfight at the expense of all his thronging memories of Spain since his first visit there. He would have liked, he said in a reminiscent mood, to have recreated all the sights and sounds and smells that had endeared Spain to him, as Goya had in paint:

> the wheat-colored fields of Navarre, the small, careful stepping
> horses . . . rope-soled shoes . . . the loops of twisted garlics;
> earthen pots; saddle bags carried across the shoulder; wine skins;
> the pitchforks made of natural wood with branches as tines; the

tall papyrus grass along the littoral; the baked clay hills, red dust, white sand. The tinny sound of churchbells in the villages; the clop of mules and burros; the rustle of the sea-wind in the palms; the smells of olive oil and dust and hot paellas and of early morning in the freshly swept cafes.[22]

He had to bring the book to an end, however. He was especially happy that for a frontispiece he had acquired an impressionistic painting of a guitar player by Juan Gris.

Hemingway was dismayed that many reviewers found *Death in the Afternoon* marred by a morbid "preoccupation with fatality" and a tendency to "he-mannish posturing."[23] But Spanish and American authorities alike considered it to be, without qualification, one of the best works on bullfighting in any language. More important to the author was the fact that in doing the bullfight book, he had organized and kept all that he had learned about Spain since his first visit there. And, as was the case with his new short story called "A Clean, Well-Lighted Place," it was clear from his exaltation of Spanish values, underlying what was ultimately a deeply tragic view of life and death, that he had been learning a great deal more about Spanish culture during the preceding ten years than merely about bullfighting.

For a while Hemingway was absent from Spain, indulging his penchant for hunting and world travel, but even in Africa he dreamed of Aragon and Navarre,[24] and during this time he was utilizing his knowledge of Spain for the background and substance of some of his best short stories. As was usual when he was away from Spain, he sought to bring Spain to him in whatever way he could. He spent much of his time with Spanish friends aboard the *Pilar*, fishing the blue waters of Key West and Bimini; and during one two-week period he spoke nothing but Spanish while they were afloat.[25] He even named his boat in honor of the shrine and the feria at Zaragoza, Spain. He regularly promoted the work of such Spanish painters and writers as Prudencio de Pereda, Joan Miró, Antonio Gattorno, Luis Quintanilla, and Juan Gris. All of this, however, was mere flirtation compared to the total commitment he was soon to make to this country he loved more than any other.

As early as 1931, at a Madrid hotel frequented by matadors, Hemingway had listened carefully to Luis Quintanilla's quiet explanation of "the necessity of revolution" in Spain, and, as he watched the power struggle build in the next few years, he knew what he would have to do when the time came. Until this time he had never shown any outstanding political allegiance, at least not in his writing. He had often said it was a mistake for a writer to take sides; but, when he looked about him and saw most of his friends turning pro-Loyalist and then saw what was happening to the Spain of many of his short stories and *The Sun Also Rises* and *Death in the Afternoon*—to the country of toreros he knew and loved—he quickly changed his stance. He was completely prepared, he said, to fight for his adopted country, Spain, though not for France.[26] He had already begun to speak of Paris in the past tense. It was "a fine place to be young in," he remarked. "A necessary part of a man's education." "But me," he said, "I now love something else. And if I fight, I fight for something else." [27] The author's commitment to the Spanish people was far too deep for him not to speak out vociferously on behalf of the salvation of democracy in Spain—his Spain.

Between the Februaries of 1937 and 1939, Hemingway made four extended journeys into the country he had called in 1926 "much the best left in Europe," but which now was threatened with wholesale destruction. And the personal fight he waged, which Scott Fitzgerald described as one of religious fervor,[28] took on a variety of forms. Hemingway not only expressed his political feelings by pledging allegiance to the Loyalists, the People's Front, but he tried to persuade the government of America to rescind its neutrality act, which forbade shipment of military equipment to Spain and thus precluded any real chance of American support for the Republican cause. Evidence of Hemingway's passionate devotion to the cause is the amount of his own material contribution. He personally raised 40,000 dollars and even went so far as to borrow money on his personal notes in order to provide the Loyalists with medical supplies. Ultimately, he accepted the presidency of the committee of the American Friends of Spanish Democracy, and in June of 1937, after two months at the Spanish Front, he delivered one of his rare political speeches at a congress of American writers in Carnegie Hall.[29]

At various times Hemingway's close friends urged him to wait out the war at home, but he replied simply that he had promised the Spaniards he would come back—that he was too deeply committed to Spain to think of taking up his life again where he had left it only a single year before.[30] From his home in Key West, he even wrote Max Perkins that he could not sleep because he knew that he belonged in Spain. One of the things he had to return to Spain for was to put the finishing touches on two films that would help raise money for Loyalist ambulances. The first of these was a documentary film called *Spain in Flames,* for which he wrote an accompanying commentary. But it was the second film, *The Spanish Earth,* designed like the first to acquaint American sympathizers with the plight of the Spanish people, that demanded his real attention. In his statement of the basic theme of this film, he revealed his main concern over the war, which was for the Spanish people themselves and for the primitive values implicit in their way of life. He wrote:

> We gained the right to cultivate our land by democratic elections.
> Now the military cliques and absentee landlords attack to take our
> land from us again. But we fight for the right to irrigate and
> cultivate this Spanish earth which the nobles kept idle for their
> own amusement.[31]

Critic Allen Guttmann argues that for Hemingway the Spanish civil war was, among other things, a fight against the spectre of an urbanized, industrialized, mechanized, and regimented world that he had managed to escape in the primitive anarchism of Spanish culture.[32] For this Hemingway constantly risked his own life in the bomb ridden hotels of besieged Madrid and in the continually shelled trenches of the International Brigade. In an early interview, he explained that his destination was Madrid, but that "he planned to visit all the nearby towns to find out what the war had done to the little people—waiters, cab drivers, cobblers, shoeshine boys." [33] In order to be as close to the common people as possible and to get a clear view of the action, he continually conducted himself more like a soldier than a noncombatant, touring the various fronts on horseback, climbing to inspect the Loyalist positions, riding in open jeeps on roads exposed to Rebel machine guns, amid the debris and struggle of flight. But these experiences, said Hemingway, sometimes seemed idyllic compared to the daily horrors of bombardment in Madrid.

Probably Hemingway's personal identification with the suffering of the Spaniards was made even more complete when the painter Luis Quintanilla, like himself a man of art, had his major paintings destroyed when a bomb gutted his studio. In answer to Hemingway's sympathetic queries, Quintanilla said, "No Ernesto, let's not talk about it. When a man loses all his life's works . . . it is much better not to talk about it." [34] The fate of Quintanilla's work, Hemingway declared, must now be classified among *los desastros de la guerra*, along with the fate of so many of his friends who had died in the war. But this was not the time for counting losses or making artistic statements about them. Like Lieutenant Colonel Gustavo Durán, former composer of music, and like Luis Quintanilla, Hemingway was an artist turned soldier, and it was now time for the man of art to be a man of action.

By the time Hemingway recognized that no further effort on his part could help postpone the loss of the Spanish Republic, it was quite clear that, despite his extensive military involvement in the war, his writer's instincts had never stopped functioning. He had, of course, written frequently and sensitively about his war experiences in feature stories for various newspapers and in spot news dispatches. His news stories invariably touched on matters of human interest and were usually enlivened by snatches of conversations with soldiers and civilians. And always prominent amid the scenes of interminable bombing and machine gun fire, the ruined cities and countryside, and the narrow misses with death was his admiration for those men who daily refused to surrender in the face of overwhelming odds. At his best Hemingway was capable of compressing into a single dispatch his sense of the ultimate tragedy the war had produced, as he did in his account of the old man at the bridge on Easter Sunday of 1938, who represented all of the war's hapless refugees. Or he could suggest with the same remarkable economy the simple courage and devotion of the common Spaniard that kept the Loyalist cause alive, as he did in his May 22, 1937 dispatch on the chauffeurs of Madrid (*B-L*, 235-40).

In addition to his reporting, Hemingway had also been carefully absorbing dramatic material for a series of short stories, a play, several poems, and a novel that was shaping up as "the fullest, the deepest, and the truest" of his novels.[35] They would all be unmistakably autobiographical, and, moreover, they would serve as further testimony to Hemingway's passionate devotion to the Spanish Republic and to his sense of oneness with the Spanish people. Nowhere in these works is the Hemingway protagonist a man apart—a mere foreign sympathizer or looker-on. Whether he is Philip Rawlings of *The Fifth Column*, Robert Jordan of *For Whom the Bell Tolls*, or the correspondent in his three best stories, "The Denunciation," "The Butterfly and the Tank," and "Night Before Battle," the protagonist is a man whose personal fate and fortunes are inextricably bound up with those of the Spanish Republic, and who even identifies certain peculiarly Spanish traits of character as his own.

Philip Rawlings not only experiences no compunction in forsaking the civilized comforts of home life—which he sees as distinctly American—when they interfere with his war efforts, but rather exalts in doing so. Robert Jordan prides himself on having "never felt like a foreigner." They accepted him completely on the basis of his "understanding the language . . . speaking it idiomatically and having a knowledge of the different places" (*FWBT, 135*). The American protagonist in the short stories takes obvious satisfaction in being thought of as a confidant of the in-group in Madrid. He is deeply involved and knowledgeable about local military matters and sees himself as a close member of a very select club.

In all of these works dealing with Hemingway's civil war experiences, the author repeatedly announces his feelings of spiritual affinity with his Spanish brothers and his continuing faith in the

primitive values inherent in their way of life. But even more important, in light of our interest in the evolution of Hemingway's Spanish
biography, is the fact that, almost in spite of himself, he begins
to evince in these works a shift in attitude toward Spain and his
fellow Spaniards. For all his Loyalist sympathies and for all his
avowed love for and allegiance to the Spanish people, it appears
that in his contact with them during the war he acquired a more
critical sense of those forces within the Spanish character that
helped first to divide the country and then to contribute to the
Loyalist defeat. It is a subtle recognition at first—one evidenced
mainly in the odor of corruption that hangs over the three civil
war stories and *The Fifth Column*. The focal point of these works,
Chicote's bar in Madrid, is described as "the best bar in the world,"
but more significantly, "a refuge from battle" (FC, 140). Here, even
the bitter conflict of war dissolves for a time, someone naively
contends. "It's funny all right," observes the protagonist of "Night
Before Battle," "with a war right down the end of the street so
you can walk to it, and then leave it and come here" (FC, 175).
But the corruption of this war and its resultant tensions—fear,
bitterness, weariness, emotional disintegration—and even death
itself have penetrated the hoped for sanctuary of Chicote's bar
and proved the speaker's words to be mere wishful thinking.

The truer, more persistent reality of these stories, as well as
of *The Fifth Column* and *For Whom the Bell Tolls*, is that the nobility
of the Loyalist cause has been severely undermined by cowardice,
suspicion, betrayal, and disunity, and that the Hemingway hero
has become increasingly bitter and callous in the wake of his
disillusionment. Hemingway attempted to sum up the fruit of his
years in war-time Spain by commenting that his visits had destroyed
his belief in an afterlife and had eliminated all his fear of death.[36]
But they had destroyed something else as well—his relatively new
belief in the ability of men of good will to combat the world's
injustice and cruelty by joining together in universal brotherhood,
and his heretofore romantic illusions about the irreproachableness
of the Spanish character. As was mentioned earlier, Hemingway
was not able at first to give voice to the disquieting insights he

had been receiving into the soul of his adopted country. He pre-
ferred to blame the results of the war on the church for having
sided with the enemy and on the cowardly machinations of corrupt,
glib politicians. Just before beginning *For Whom the Bell Tolls*, he
commented "with a mixture of sadness and scorn" about "the
carnival of treachery and rottenness on both sides" of the conflict
in Spain, adding that he believed "the politicians were treacherously
at work behind the scenes." [37] But ultimately he worried that something more profound, more deeply primitive—a tendency to anarchistic rebellion and arrogant individualism—had predetermined
the tragic consequences of the war. It only remained for Robert
Jordan, during one of his soul-searing delvings into the darker
motivations of his comrades' behavior, to identify the strange,
unsettling emotional paradox within the Spaniard's character that
caused him to turn on you as "they always turned on everyone"
(*FWBT*, 135). "There is no finer and no worse people in the world,"
Jordan concludes.

For Whom the Bell Tolls was Hemingway's farewell to Spain for
many years—years, observes Carlos Baker, that marked the author's
greatest period of creative inactivity.[38] Partly because the Second
World War drew on all his energies, but mainly because of his
leftist political leanings during the Spanish civil war, he did not
return for some years to the country where Franco now ruled. It
was a painful and self-imposed exile—painful because, despite
whatever loss of illusion Hemingway might have suffered as the
result of his war experiences, Spain was the country he continually
traveled back to for an uplift of spirit. He still insisted that his
efforts during the war on the behalf of the Spanish Republic had
revived and rejuvenated him, and many critics argued that those
experiences had given him a new lease on life as a writer. In 1940,
looking back on the spring of 1937, Hemingway said that "the
period of fighting when we thought that the Republic could win
was the happiest period of our lives." [39]

True to his custom over the years, if the author could not be
in Spain, he could do the next best thing by remaining in constant
contact with Spanish friends and with various forms of Spanish

culture. He could, for instance, establish a home at the big Spanish style farm at Finca Vigia in Cuba. Here at San Francisco de Paula, just outside Havana, he could inhabit a piece of Spain and live in semi-primitive seclusion from the civilized world. And even then, he would continuously have the company of such favorite Spanish friends as Don Andrés Untzaín, a Catholic priest who had served as a machine gunner for the Loyalists; Gustavo Durán, whom he called the real hero of *For Whom the Bell Tolls;* a group of anti-Fascist Spanish noblemen then living in voluntary exile in Cuba; and a number of Cuban fishermen and waiters. Some of these people he enlisted for service aboard the *Pilar* as espionage agents in a counterintelligence operation that had a distinctly Spanish flavor to it. Loaded with its group of assorted Spaniards, bazookas, grenades, and machine guns, the *Pilar* attempted to head off German submarines then preying on allied tankers and cargo ships throughout the Caribbean. Even his major literary endeavor during this time was accomplished in a Spanish atmosphere. During the time he was writing *Across The River And Into The Trees,* he said that he had taken his favorite Goya and El Greco down from the walls and leaned them against chairs in his bedroom so that they would be the first objects he would see when he awoke at dawn.[40] He later commented, too, that the pictures in the Prado were "as solidly etched" in his "head and heart" as if they had hung on the walls of the Finca in all the years since he had last seen them.[41]

During this time, Hemingway explained that he grew away from spectator sports, and that his attitude toward bullfighters altered somewhat "because he suffered too much vicariously when they succumbed to fear;" to gorings, or death; he even resolved never to have a bullfighter for a friend again. But a close friend of his, an established *aficionado* named Charles Wertenbaker, observed in 1944 that Hemingway was as possessive about bulls and bullfighting as ever—as "if he had staked out a personal claim which others could invade at their peril." [42] And the bullfight as metaphor was still as active in his creative imagination as ever. In a war poem called "Poem to Mary," in which he bitterly recounts the stupidities of war and the nightmare of battle between the midnights of

September 13 and 14, 1944, he resurrected his old analogy about ritualistic death in the bullring as compared to the chaotic slaughter of war. In still another instance, he utilized the analogy in a different way to justify his enjoyment of killing the Nazis and the Fascists during the war. A man could assert his manhood by killing and being killed, he believed.[43] As a passionate exponent of blood sports all his adult life, he had learned well the "aesthetic pleasure and pride" that came from "killing cleanly." Not for nothing, he said, had he watched the destruction of 1,500 bulls in the ten years before the publication of *Death in the Afternoon.*

Hemingway's last close association with a bullfighter had been with Sidney Franklin in 1937 when, despite the seriousness of the situation in Madrid, his enthusiasm for bullfighting took momentary precedence. He went almost daily to Franklin's room to admire the matador's bullfight paraphernalia. Even though Franklin moved gingerly because of a recent goring, he would proudly unpack his collection of matador costumes and swords for Hemingway to gaze upon and handle. Then, invariably, the two men would have to vent their excitement by acting out the *corrida* in the hotel room. Franklin would seize a cape, crying out "Toro—huh—toro," and perform a series of passes on Hemingway who, grinning happily, had put his hands to his ears to simulate horns and was lunging at the matador. The two men kept up a breathless commentary in the slang of the Spanish bullring.[44] Now, over a decade later, Hemingway was ready again to adopt another young bullfighter through whom he could revitalize himself as man and artist.

Nearly thirty years after the events recorded in *The Sun Also Rises,* Hemingway returned to Spain in the summer of 1953 seeking the delights which had so moved him earlier—desperately trying to go home again to where he felt more at ease with himself than anywhere else. Franco was still in power at the time, and Hemingway's Loyalist sympathies were well-known, but his friends agreed that his return was honorable so long as he did not compromise his original views and kept clear of politics. Hemingway, himself, observed that "it had required great *cojones* to reenter Franco's Spain," and took pleasure in stressing the danger he had been in.[45] The narrative record of this return, *The Dangerous Summer*, tells about "the usual rough seven days" at the Pamplona fiesta. But more important, it is flooded with nostalgic reflections of an old man who has indeed come home again.

Hemingway said, "It was strange going back to Spain again . . . the country that I loved more than any other . . . we came back to Spain and it seemed too good to be true." (*DS*, 49: 17) The days in Spain were so beautiful, he wrote a friend, that he felt as if he had already died and gone to heaven. He took special pleasure in showing Mary Hemingway the landscape of *For Whom the Bell Tolls* and said he was satisfied to discover that he had described the terrain exactly as it was.[46] He was equally pleased with his reception in Pamplona, where he was treated, he said, "like local boy makes good." It moved him greatly that bulls were dedicated to him on two successive days. "The crowd stood up and roared its plaudits," Carlos Baker reports. "Hundreds of people brought him bullfight tickets to be autographed, and he reveled in these signs that he was still revered by the Spaniards." [47] On another occasion, thousands of people cheered him after a brilliant performance by a young bullfighter named Segura. The matador was awarded both ears of his bull when Hemingway formally recognized his performance by waving a salute to the President.[48] In turn, Hemingway did his part to restore old ties and acknowledge his indebtedness to the Spanish people by insisting upon staying in the Hotel Florida, where he had lived in 1937. He must do this, he said, because he knew the Spaniards would regard this as "the correct thing for him to do." [49]

The brightest event of his return to Spain in 1953 was his first meeting with a young matador named Antonio Ordóñez, a son of Niño de la Palma, whom the author had painted in a memorable portrait as the young bullfighter-hero Pedro Romero. Hemingway explained that his purpose in coming back to Spain was to get more material for an appendix to *Death in the Afternoon* on the evolution and decline of the modern bullfight. But Antonio's performances soon convinced him not only that decline was too strong a word, but that Ordóñez was far better than his father had been on his father's best day.[50] He said that he found it difficult to concentrate on anyone or anything besides Antonio, whom he described as "brave, smart, fast, loving," and "incorruptible in a corrupt sport," and as "the best guy you'll ever meet."[51] His spirits were rejuvenated by Ordóñez as they had been by Sidney Franklin and the other matadors before him, and nothing would do until he had begun his new study of the bullfight in the atmosphere of Antonio's heroic performances and while he was still inside "the magical borders of Spain."[52]

Successive visits to Spain in 1954, 1956, 1959, and 1960, when he visited familiar and pleasurable haunts—beloved towns, cafes, hotels—attempting to restore himself as man and writer, deepened his paternal friendship with the young Ordóñez and led to his account of the intensé rivalry between Ordóñez and Luis Miguel Dominguin, another matador of great prowess. Quite clearly, Ordóñez, "this dark young Spanish athlete, lithe as a panther, brave as a lion, a genuine champion in his profession," had become for Hemingway another symbol of the way he himself wanted to be—the embodiment of perfect manhood. Hemingway claimed that Ordóñez was as dependent on him for spiritual nourishment as he was on Ordóñez. "Antonio wants me with him all the time," Hemingway declared, "as we are a winning combination."[53] Antonio's grueling schedule took its toll on Hemingway. It was as nerve shattering as "being married to an alcoholic," he said. But he gloried in being seen in Antonio's presence and insisted that it was absolutely necessary to his friend's well-being that he be with him at each fight.[54]

In the last, long-suffering years of Hemingway's life—1954 to 1960—his creative energies were so worn down by problems of ill-health, staggering income-tax bills, political conditions in Cuba that threatened the destruction of his home at the Finca, and extreme nervous depression, spurred on by the fear that time for him was growing short, that he felt he could no longer sustain his writing. But, as he had said so often, he claimed that, in having Spain to travel back to as "home base for a quiet place to write and to rest up between bullfights," he still had one sure cure for ill-health and waning spirits.[55] In just such a positive state of mind, he determined to finish his final tribute to Spain, *The Dangerous Summer*, at La Consula, close to the village of Coín near Malaga on the Costa del Sol.

There is a strong possibility—as will be argued later in this study—that the author's desire to return to Spain in time of stress—especially the emotional stress of his last years—contains an element of tragic irony. That rather than help cure or alleviate the emotional problems that depleted the author's creative energy and led up to his death, his experiences in Spain may have encouraged and exacerbated them. In writing a letter in Spanish to Juanito Quintana, Hemingway complained that the pressure of working on *The Dangerous Summer* had exhausted his eyes, but worst of all his head. All this forced labor *(trabajando forzado)*, he wrote, has confused my brain—if not something more serious.[56]

The "something more serious" had been manifesting itself in a variety of irrationally aggressive actions ever since the close of the Spanish civil war. At that time Hemingway had described himself as "self-righteous, intolerant, ruthless and cruel." [57] In the years to follow, his self-characterization was corroborated more and more by those around him. Friends observed that he had become increasingly arrogant, belligerent, and boastful, and that he was more than ever before full of self-dramatization, with a curious liking for obsequious behavior among his admirers.[58] He had even grown pathologically suspicious of those closest to him and was given to sudden acts of cruelty toward those he feared or resented.

There is a strong basis for believing that much of Hemingway's aggressively adolescent behavior during the last few years of his life can be explained, in part, as the ultimate product of his years in Spain. As a measure of the impact Spain was having on his thinking during the years of *The Sun Also Rises*, Hemingway had declared, much in the manner of Jake Barnes, "Gradually you form your own ideas of how you should lead your life. It's strange, but when you get hurt—really hurt, I mean—you're willing to throw those ideas aside for another set that now make sense to you and calm your hurt." [59] What this "hurt" was exactly is the subject of the next chapter. It was one that caused him to view the universe as endlessly hostile and unjust—a view central to what he came to appreciate as the Spaniard's "commonsense" approach to life and death. And, further, because of such a world-view and because he shared with the Spanish matador certain "coincidences of spirit," as Castillo-Puche puts it—a temperamental accord with a profound anarchism as its base—Hemingway adjudged the matador's aggressive stance to be a correct and necessary one for survival.

Not long after Hemingway had seen his first bullfight, he had taught his infant son "to put up his fists and assume a ferocious expression," as if, like the matador, he might steel himself against and intimidate his opponent by manufacturing a tough exterior. The problem with such a stance, or disguise, as Castillo-Puche observed during his years of close contact with Hemingway, was that the mask—the "ferocious expression"—had in Hemingway's case finally become the man, at least in popular view, and that the author's truer inner-self—that which was basically humane, suffering, and solitary—had become tragically suppressed. Friends and critics alike remarked that the final results of Hemingway's success seemed to be that he had come, in his later years, to sound distressingly like his fictional heroes—more and more like his own idea of how he should be. Andrew Turnbull thought, for instance, that the author's actions had become "staged and put on," and referred to his "sad mask of a face." [60] But no one saw that this fictional mask, this "mask of histrionics" as Castillo-Puche calls it, with its "evasion" and its "flex of exhibitionism," had a distinctly Spanish look to it, and that it contained the final, revelatory truth about Hemingway's personal Spanish tragedy. It was at once the symbol and consequence of the author's emotional and artistic commitment to what he viewed as the Spaniard's *particularismo*—his intensely individualistic and bellicose nature—which remained profoundly with him until the moment of his death, his own "moment of truth."

"My idea of heaven is a big bullring where I have two permanent barrera seats," Hemingway said in 1925.

This lead story in the *Toronto Star Weekly,* which reflects Hemingway's early interest in the bullfight as a symbol of life and death, has been reproduced by William White in *By-Line: Ernest Hemingway.*

23

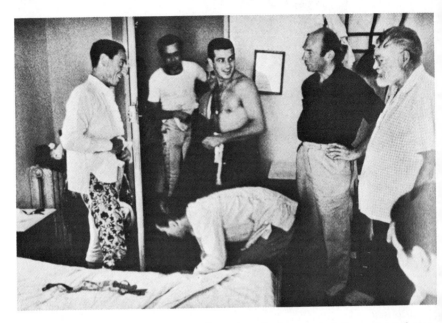

Throughout his life, Hemingway took pride and pleasure in being accepted into the close circle of his bullfighting friends, and he considered the time of preparation for the fight to be deadly serious. Here, much like Jake Barnes in *The Sun Also Rises*, he looks solemnly on as Dominguin and Ordóñez, the world's leading matadors in 1959, dress for a fight.

Here Hemingway shows Sidney Franklin killing with "sangfroid" on the day of his debut in Sevilla, and also making a veronica with classic grace and with no contortions.

Hemingway uses these pictures of Nicanor Villalta in *Death in the Afternoon* to show the basis of emotion in bullfighting. Hemingway says, "The emotion is given by the closeness with which the matador brings the bull past his body and it is prolonged by the slowness with which he can execute the pass." Villalta is so good, Hemingway says, that, after the bull goes by, if there is no blood on the matador's belly, you ought to get your money back.

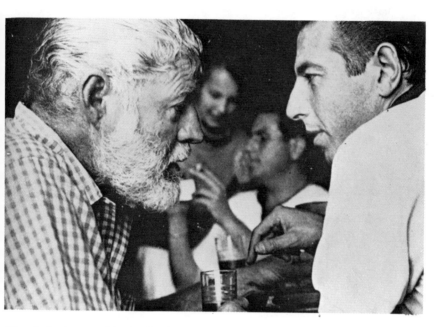

The "winning combination" of Hemingway and Ordóñez. Hemingway claimed that the matador was as dependent on him for spiritual nourishment as he was on Ordóñez.

Both pictures convey the author's determination to try his hand at being a matador at the yearly "amateurs" in the Pamplona fiesta.

TORONTO WRITER GORED BY ANGRY BULL IN SPAIN
Ernest Hemingway, formerly foreign correspondent of The Toronto Star and member of the local staff, was recently gored by an angry bull, during the annual fiesta at Pamplona, Spain. He received only painful bruises from the bull's bandaged horns, while his companion, Donald Ogden Stewart, an American newspaper correspondent, suffered two broken ribs. Above is shown Mr. Hemingway, with his wife, who is in Europe with him.

BULL GORES TORONTO WRITER IN ANNUAL PAMPLONA FIESTA

But Only Badly Bruised — Companion, However, Had Two Ribs Broken—Ernest Hemingway Recently on the Staff of The Star

Special to The Star by United Press

Paris, July 20.—Two young American writers from the colony here were gored by a bull at Pamplona, Spain, during the course of the annual fiesta.

A party of four, consisting of Donald Ogden Stewart, Ernest Hemingway, Robert McAlmon and John Dos Passos (author of "Soldiers Three"), left here some time ago for a Spanish tour having Pamplona as its chief objective. At that place it is the custom every year to drive a herd of bulls through the barricaded street to the arena. The animals are pursued by the youth of the town, who later bait and fight them in the bull ring, without using any weapons. Escape from injury depends upon the youths' agility.

Both Stewart and Hemingway participated in the first day of the sports without meeting mishap. On the second, however, Stewart was thrown by a bull, but, undaunted, wagered Hemingway he could return, ride the wild beast, blow smoke in its eyes and finally wrestle and throw it.

When he was preparing to launch upon this enterprise, a toreador presented him with a red cape. Before he had finished shaking hands with his Spanish backer, a bull had charged him, hoisted him on its horns, rolled him over and finally hurled him into the air. When he crashed down the enraged animal tried to gore him.

Hemingway ran to the rescue and was also gored but, owing to the fact that the bulls used in this annual carnival have their horns bandaged, he suffered only painful bruises. Stewart had two ribs broken.

Ernest Hemingway is familiar to readers of The Toronto Star through European cables and correspondence which he has contributed to this paper. He covered the Genoa and Lausanne conferences for The Star and interviewed many of the most prominent statesmen of Europe. Last autumn and winter he was here in this city working on the staff of The Toronto Daily Star and later The Star Weekly.

Mr. Hemingway, who is a son of Dr. C. E. Hemingway, 600 North Kenilworth avenue, Oak Park, Chicago, served during the war as a lieutenant with the A. E. F. in Italy. He was the first American wounded on that front and was awarded two war crosses and a silver medal.

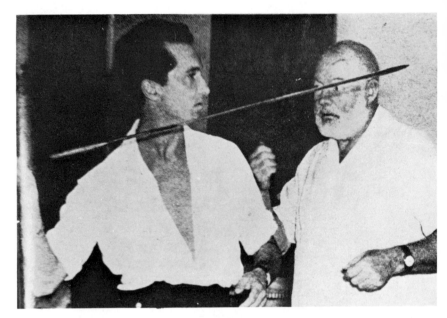

Always fascinated with bullfighting technique, Hemingway takes lessons from Luis Miguel Dominguin (above) and then demonstrates his own form with the cape for Dominguin and Ava Gardner (below).

It was Maera's arrogant indomitability that Hemingway admired most about him. In the picture above Hemingway asks the reader to focus his attention on the fact that the matador works in an increasingly dangerous and seemingly impossible terrain—that he performs "perfectly in the manner and terrain that he chose." Below, he exhibits the reckless stance before death, in the form of the charging bull, that made him a perfect model for the author's last four protagonists.

2 / Why Spain? The Early Hero

ERNEST HEMINGWAY once stated, "No man can reveal me to the world more vividly than I have chosen to reveal myself. . . . I tell people all about myself in my books." [1] For a long time critics have been aware of the autobiographical nature of Hemingway's work. A number of studies have shown how he wove the most important events in his own life into the fabric of his fiction, and how much in common he had with his fictional heroes. Personal interviews with Hemingway, such as those conducted by George Plimpton and Lillian Ross, have particularly underscored the theory that the feelings and attitudes of Hemingway's protagonists can be identified as his own.

More recently, accounts of Hemingway's personal attitudes and behavioral patterns by Leicester Hemingway, Morley Callaghan, Carlos Baker, A. E. Hotchner, and Philip Young have illustrated more dramatically than ever before the extent to which the author projected himself—his problems and viewpoints—into the lives of his literary creations. Philip Young has said, "It would be hard to think of even an autobiographical writer (Thomas Wolfe, for instance) who gave a more exact account of his own experience and of his own personality in the guise of prose fiction." [2] "Since 1924," Young tells us, "he had been writing out the story of one man who was based on himself. . . . The experiences of childhood, adolescence and young manhood which shape Nick Adams shaped as well Lt. Henry, Jake Barnes, Col. Cantwell, and several other heroes. They all have had Nick's childhood, Nick's adolescence, Nick's young manhood." [3]

In his investigation of the various points of correspondence between Hemingway's own life and that of his heroes, Young concentrates particularly on the writer's traumatic contacts with death and violence in his early environment and on the damage inflicted upon the author by the shock of war, all of which Hemingway wrote about in his first stories and novels. Stressing the importance of the wound Hemingway suffered in World War I, which he contends left permanent scars, visible and otherwise, Young shows that much of what Hemingway wrote after the wound reads like a therapeutic process in which he tried to exorcise his fears by writing them out on paper; and, furthermore, that the war injury evidently culminated, climaxed, and epitomized the wounds he had been receiving as a growing boy. From here on in, he observes, the Hemingway hero is a wounded man, wounded not only physically but—as soon becomes apparent—psychically as well.[4]

A brief review of Young's position provides a logical starting point. Primarily it helps to establish that the young Hemingway hero—a man suffering from shock as the result of his early exposures to aggression—is a far different person than the Spanish-derived or Spanish-oriented protagonists of Hemingway's later work. But it also allows meaningful speculation—insofar as the early hero's attitudes and problems can be accepted as the author's own—that just such a condition caused the author, as a defensive measure, to align himself with the primitive and militant laws and forces within the world of the *corrida*.[5]

Since the psychologically crippling events of Hemingway's early boyhood can be said to have "climaxed" and "culminated" in his war experience, his account of that confrontation as it is described in *A Farewell To Arms* and through the character of Frederick Henry provides the clearest definition of the dilemma and attitudes characteristic of the early hero. The war for Tenente Henry is, indeed, a shattering experience that mutilates his body and confounds his reason. Throughout the novel, his life and everything he holds dear is threatened by misunderstanding, betrayal, and death. Ultimately, the barbarism of war and the biological treachery of childbirth destroy his relationship with Catherine and force upon him a totally fatalistic view of his place in the universe.

Catherine's death is merely the climax of endless scenes of dying, mutilation, and emotional confusion that wear indelibly on Henry's mind. With growing despair and subsequent emotional withdrawal, he watches soldiers who die from cholera or from self-mutilation, the degeneration of his close friend Rinaldi, and the misguided execution of officers by their own men, all of which epitomizes for Henry the brutal senselessness of war, and finally the agonized childbirth undergone by Catherine.

At first Henry is only bewildered and stunned by the terrible sense of injustice, which he does not understand or at least cannot cope with. He has learned that war is a dirty business, and, by the time his own involvement in it comes to an end, he has learned to discern "liars that lie to nations" and is thoroughly disillusioned with the "glorious conflict." He says at one point:

> I was always embarrassed by the words sacred, glorious, and sacrifice and the expression in vain. We had heard them sometimes standing in the rain almost out of earshot, so that only the shouted words came through, and had read them, on proclamations, now for a long time, and I had seen nothing sacred, and the things that were glorious had no glory and the sacrifices were like the stockyards at Chicago if nothing was done with the meat except to bury it. There were many words that you could not stand to hear and finally only the names of the places . . . were all you could say and have them mean anything. Abstract words such as glory, honor, courage or hallow were obscene beside the concrete names of villages, the numbers of roads, the names of rivers, the numbers of regiments and the dates. (*FA,* 191)

Henry's response to the cruel affair of war amounts, however, to more than mere disenchantment with the ideals for which the war has been fought. By the end of the novel, his fear of annihilation has become so overbearing and omnipresent that he states his predicament in terms of a conspiracy, which for some inexplicable reason exists to destroy and humiliate him. In what is perhaps the most oft quoted passage of the novel, Henry says:

> If people bring so much courage to this world the world has to
> kill them to break them so of course it kills them. . . . It kills the
> very good and the very gentle and the very brave impartially. If
> you are none of these you can be sure it will kill you too but
> there will be no special hurry. (FA, 258, 259)

His own wound and the death that threatens Catherine cause him
to believe that there is simply no defense against the great and
final foe—death. "Now Catherine would die," he despairingly concludes. "That was what you did" (FA, 338).

Shocked by the horrors of battle and of Catherine's death, life
appears to Henry at the end of the novel as an endless trap, deadly
and treacherous. All relationships seem inevitably to run the same
course; all are doomed to failure because they are liable to all
the accidents of a world in which human beings are like ants
running back and forth on a log burning in a campfire and in
which death is "just a dirty trick" (FA, 342). Henry's final protest
against the impersonal "they" that sets and springs the trap that
snares and kills is embodied in these words:

> They threw you in and told you the rules and the first time they
> caught you off base they killed you. Or they killed you
> gratuitously like Aymo. Or gave you the syphilis like Rinaldi. But
> they killed you in the end. You could count on that. (FA, 350)

This is the fatalistic note on which the novel ends. Cut off from
his relationship with Catherine by the mysterious "they" that
pursued them to Switzerland, Henry goes out into the rain of a
chaotic and meaningless world feeling himself the victim of a
horrible injustice. He postulates that what happened to Catherine
can happen to anyone and was beyond his control. She did not
deserve to die, but the universe does not care. It kills the brave
as well as the good. In short, life is viewed only as an endless
destruction.

This pattern of endless hostility, fear, and frustration—of the
good man perpetually threatened with annihilation and emotionally
disabled by fear and cynicism—is the dominant strain in Hemingway's work before the writing of A Farewell To Arms and up to

that of *Death In The Afternoon.* Everywhere in the early Nick Adams stories is encountered the thesis that life is a conspiracy to break and destroy the aspiring individual. Malcolm Cowley has likened the world of Nick Adams to "a hostile forest, full of unseen dangers," in which death spies on him from every tree.[6] Just as with Frederick Henry, Nick is trapped and preyed upon by a malicious world that refuses to make sense. Also like Henry, Nick becomes the inwardly passive victim of a meaningless determinism and the emotional inertia and impotence it breeds.

Life for Nick Adams, like the assassins in "The Killers," has no mercy; it steadily and relentlessly drives the defenseless individual into an impasse like that of Ole Andreson, who simply accepts his death by lying down and waiting for his executioners. "There isn't anything I can do about it," says Andreson, lying on his bed and turning his face fatalistically to the wall (*SS*, 287). Despite Nick's efforts to help Ole avoid his fate, he finds that there is nothing he can do about it either. When he reports the situation back in the lunchroom where he first encountered the killers, he says: "I'm going to get out of this town. I can't stand to think about him waiting in the room and knowing he's going to get it. It's too damned awful" (*SS*, 289).

Nick's early environment is filled with similar contacts with death and aggression that make him painfully aware of his own vulnerability. In "The Battler" Nick runs into a former boxing champion and is stunned to find him beaten and misshapen, traveling around the country with his Negro companion. He has taken too many beatings, the Negro explains. Then Nick hears the sordid story of the way the ex-fighter's reputation had been smeared by his enemies, and as the story ends Nick, again, is dazed and bewildered in the face of his new knowledge that the good and the brave are the first to be betrayed and destroyed. His response is to draw within himself with only his fears for company, and then to take to his heels.

"The Killers" and "The Battler" were probably the result of Hemingway's early experience bumming around the country, riding in freight cars, and sleeping in hobo jungles. But in writing about the blind cruelty of sexual instinct in "Up In Michigan," the physical breakdown and active cruelty of man in "The Doctor And The Doctor's Wife" and "Indian Camp," Hemingway reveals that the threat of aggression was also active in his Michigan childhood. Nick's early life is torn by the vision of his mother sitting home with her Bible, in a pious, smug, middle-class background, a copy of *Science And Health* on the table, and the stale, provincial atmosphere it provides. Nick harbors a grudge against his mother because she seems oblivious to the naturalistic struggle raging around her. In the story, "The Doctor And The Doctor's Wife," Nick finds his mother totally unaware of the Indians wrangling with Doc Adams about logs he is supposed to have stolen. His mother's religion blinds her to the hostility around them, and Nick shows his disdain by going off to the woods with his father where it is cool to hunt squirrels. In contrast to his mother, Nick feels he understands the life of a man and knows the remorse his father is suffering for having backed down from a fight with big Dick Boulton. He has decided that one must be hard in life, that only the toughskinned survive, and, though he is sorry for his father's lack of courage and painfully conscious of its absence, this is still less a threat to him than his mother's priggishness and talkativeness. Years later, Nick, in the character of Robert Jordan, is still brooding over his father's lack of backbone. "He was just a coward and that was the worst luck any man could have. Because if he wasn't a coward he would have stood up to the woman and not let her bully him" (*FWBT*, 339).

Because of his mother, Nick seems sour on women in general and does not want what happened to his father to happen to him. He was weak and sentimental, and, like most sentimental people, he was abused. All sentimental people are betrayed. Ultimately, this abuse leads his father to take his life, and Nick decides: "He had much bad luck, and it was not all of it his own. He had died in a trap that he had helped only a little to set" (*SS*, 489, 490).

Because domesticity is seen as a further threat and destroyer of manhood, Nick resists being tied down. Marrying and settling down represent the stifling of soul, the spiritual death that every

Hemingway hero abhors. "Once a man's married, he's absolutely bitched," a friend tells Nick reassuringly in "The Three-Day Blow." "He hasn't got anything more. Nothing. Not a damn thing. He's done for. You've seen the guys that get married" (SS, 122). The two boys in this story are talking about Nick's break-up with his girl in "The End Of Something." Suddenly, for Nick, everything was over between Marge and him. He had become disenchanted with young love. "All of a sudden everything was over," Nick said, "I don't know why it was. I couldn't help it. Just like when the three day blows come now and rip all the leaves off the trees" (SS, 123). Nick is sad at first and partly condemns himself, but his friend assures him that marriage in this case would have been treacherous. "If you'd have married her you would have had to marry the whole family. Remember her mother and that guy she married" (SS, 122). Nick feels that he loses something no matter which way he commits himself, but prefers flight to the complexity of domestic life. And finally he reconciles himself to the pessimistic belief that "That's the way it works out," that nothing lasts forever. He tells himself, "outside now the Marge business was no longer so tragic. It was not even very important. The wind blew everything like that away." And so comes the end of Nick's romantic notions. Love ends just as suddenly and without warning as "when the three-day blows come and rip all the leaves off the trees" (SS, 125). It, too, becomes a questionable value, which the hero learns to degrade in a way that verges on mania.

From here on out the Hemingway hero views women—especially Anglo-Saxon women—as a definite destructive force. The fear that a woman will get him down or lure him into some kind of self-betrayal becomes one of the major antagonisms he must guard against. He must not get in a position where he can be taken advantage of.

A variety of other stories illustrate this pattern of entrapment and frustration in a meaningless and hostile world. Decline and finally defeat, as epitomized in the fate of Frederick Henry, are encountered without sufficient reason, consolation, or escape. These stories are filled with the apprehension of being ensnared by some insidious tentacle of the omnipresent "they," or losing control of oneself and hence becoming subject to the "double cross" or some other form of breach of faith. In "My Old Man," the protagonist is forced to ride in "fixed" races. The second time he races, he breaks his neck going over the water jump and is brought in dead. And one observer notes: "Seems like when they get started they don't leave a guy nothing." In "The Three-Day Blow," two boys, who are eager sportsmen, talk of unscrupulous trades and baseball monopolies that have ruined many good athletes, and they note that one year the "Cards" lost their chance for the pennant because of a train wreck just at the time they were going well. In "Fifty Grand," in the last fight of his principled career, Jack Brennan finds himself involved in a sordid "fix" and is forced to commit a foul in order to retain his integrity. In "A Pursuit Race," Billy Campbell has shot himself full of dope to put a screen between himself and life's treacheries. Everything eventually lets you down, he concludes. "If you love women," he says, "you'll get a dose . . . if you love horses——" (SS, 354). His fatalistic view of things is summed up in his comment to his manager: "They haven't got a cure for anything" (SS, 353).

All of these stories indicate Hemingway's obsession with all that threatens to destroy. Otherwise normal individuals are depicted as baited and persecuted to the point of exhaustion. The world without is painted in colors unceasingly hostile and unsympathetic to the good man's ideals. And the author's emphasis is on the individual's recognition that such a world exists and that, indeed, there is no cure for it.

Yet another set of stories deals not so much with the destructive things that happen to people and the ways in which they happen as with the attempt to find defensive structures by which the brave and simple man might survive in such a world. I would place the novel *The Sun Also Rises* and the stories "In Another Country," "Soldier's Home," and "Big Two-Hearted River" in this category. In these are shown what the suffering of the war has cost the Hemingway hero, but also what resistances and defenses his creator has learned to put up. More importantly, they indicate that

Hemingway's emotional situation after the war, which Young has shown to be also that of his heroes, created in him a psychological readiness to react to Spain in the way he did. His close acquaintance with aggression not only lost him his sleep for a long while, but it made him a different man—a man who looked to the primitive environment of Spain for a new sense of meaning and purpose.

3 / Intimations of Spain: The Hero's Search for Another Country

IN THE spring of 1919 Hemingway went back to Oak Park, Illinois with the medals and other souvenirs he had won at the Italian front, including his new aluminum kneecap, a grafted bone in his foot, and various pieces of scrap-metal that the surgeons had been unable to remove. The story of his return home is recorded in "Soldier's Home" and "Big Two-Hearted River." But as Young has amply demonstrated, the author's period of convalescence and adjustment after the war is also written about in "A Way You'll Never Be," "Now I Lay Me," "In Another Country," and *The Sun Also Rises*.

Each of these stories looks backward to the wound that Hemingway received in the war; the hero is either still in uniform or just recently out, and in each case he bears the marks of the author who for a long time after his wounding in Italy in 1918 could not sleep with the light out.[1] In "Now I Lay Me," the hero says: "If I could have a light I was not afraid to sleep, because I knew my soul would only go out of me if it were dark" (*SS*, 367). To occupy his sleepless nights, he talks to an orderly about his condition since his wound and lies awake thinking about the other, less visible woundings he has been receiving since childhood. At one point he thinks to himself:

> I myself did not want to sleep because I had been living for a
> long time with the knowledge that if I ever shut my eyes in the
> dark and let myself go, my soul would go out of my body. I had
> been blown up at night and felt it go out of me, and go off and

41

then come back. I tried never to think about it, but it had started to go since, in the nights, just at the moment of going off to sleep, and I could only stop it by a very great effort. (*SS*, 363)

In "A Way You'll Never Be," his memories of the wounding have brought him beyond insomnia to the edge of insanity. And as the title of the story suggests, things can never be the same again. Further symptoms of the hero's condition of prolonged shock are delineated in "Big Two-Hearted River" and "Soldier's Home." In both stories he is shown as a deeply hurt man, and in keeping with the general behavioral pattern of the early heroes, he is on the defensive and withdraws as much as possible from experience. "Soldier's Home," especially, shows precisely the way the hero can never be again. His attempt to immerse himself in the old familiar but now hopelessly alien patterns of home life proves unsuccessful, and he is alienated from the conventional, middle-class American town to which he has returned. For a while he lives alone, without complications, attachments, and responsibilities, but soon he grows tired of the little restrictions and pettinesses of normal life, a life operating under the usual conventions and restrictions that seem silly to him after what he has been through. He finds it repugnant when his mother asks him to kneel by her side and pray God to make him a good boy again (*SS*, 152). The contrast between her honeyed talk and the things that happened in the trenches of Fossalta nauseates him; he recognizes that nothing in her life has allowed her to glimpse the tragic side of life and the inevitability of death that he learned about in the war. He admits that only when he is with other soldiers who have shared his experiences, when "he fell into the easy pose of the old soldier among other soldiers" (*SS*, 148), can he feel at all comfortable. He concludes that "here at home it was all too complicated," and resolves to make his life as simple as possible.

This last point is of major relevance. In the stories dealing with Hemingway's experience before and during the war, the hero is so emotionally disabled by what he sees that flight becomes his response. But in the present set of stories, the author depicts his hero as undergoing a period of quiet stock-taking during which his protection-seeking instinct leads him in a new direction. His dominant impulse is to simplify things as much as possible, to play a solitary game, and to immerse himself in the simple, primitive pleasures, such as fishing, eating, and drinking. He must keep physically occupied, keep his hands busy; he must not think or he will be unable to sleep. He must learn to keep his emotions in check and, above all, to avoid complexity.

For the moment, the hero is a man without a country, without religion, without relation to any cultural or national past, and without ideological relation to the future. The only thing he is sure of is that a life in America is impossible for him. "Here at home it was all too complicated," the protagonist in "Soldier's Home" concludes (SS, 148). In "Now I Lay Me," the recuperating soldier thinks of going home again to America but is soon put off by painful recollections of the domestic complications between his mother and father. The thought of going home and settling down appears ominous to him. At the end of the story he remarks about the orderly who has been encouraging him to go home and marry: "He was going back to America and he was very certain about marriage and knew it would fix up everything" (SS, 371).

"In Another Country" might be said to have a pivotal position in the present set of stories because it represents the life Hemingway rejected as well as his search for a new sense of direction. As Carlos Baker suggests, the "other country" in the story is Italy, but it is also a country where a man can find things he cannot lose.[2] The hero is taking treatments for his wounded leg along with an Italian major whose hand has withered from a wound and whose wife has died of pneumonia. Through his conversations with the major, Nick comes to realize that his plan to return to the United States to marry and resume a normal life is out of the question. The major calls him a fool and explains, as a result of bitter experience, why a man should not marry:

> He cannot marry, he said angrily. If he is to lose everything, he should not place himself in a position to lose that. He should not place himself in a position to lose. He should find things he cannot lose. (SS, 271)

Soon the hero would go to Paris, and then to Spain, in search of a country where a man can find things he cannot lose and where he might bind his wounds. But first, one more story in this set depicts the hero's separation from his old life and his search for a new habitat. In "Big Two-Hearted River," Hemingway clearly foreshadows his interest in the pattern of ritualized, primitive-defensive behavior that attracts him so strongly to Spain. Malcolm Cowley says that the hero's whole fishing expedition in this story "might be regarded as an incantation, a spell to banish evil spirits." [3] The trip, indeed, seems to offer Nick the restorative agents necessary for his return to health. It is characterized by order, cleanliness, and simplicity, and its effect is therapeutic. Nick becomes immersed in the sights, sounds, smells, and tastes of a kind of primitivistic wonderland and feels that the war is finally behind him. "He felt that he had left everything behind him. . . . It was all back of him" (SS, 210).

The cool stream, the clean air, the fresh smells contrast with the artificiality of urban life and the chaos of war. And occupying himself with the business of the trip, he manages to keep ugly memories at bay. Nick goes through each step of the process of camping and fishing in an instinctively rhythmic manner. He finds the same sense of emotional satisfaction in performing these simple, primitive rites as Jake Barnes soon experiences through the ritualized and ceremonial pattern of the bullfight.

The hero's period of quiet stock-taking continues in The Sun Also Rises. Just as in "In Another Country" and "Big Two-Hearted River," the hero has been gravely wounded, physically and psychically, during the war. Any doubt that this is the same man should be dispelled when we learn that he, too, cannot sleep without a light: "For six months I never slept with the electric light off," Jake says (SB, 148). Jake's world is still a world at war—if not now in the literal sense, certainly in the constant fight against despair and personal dissolution. It is a world, Jake Barnes has concluded, where "everybody behaves badly, give them the proper chance" (SR, 181). But just as in these previous stories, rather than give in to despair, the hero attempts to learn how to live in the world that has crippled him. "Perhaps as you went along you did learn something," Jake says. "I did not care what it was all about. All I wanted to know was how to live in it. Maybe if you found out how to live in it you learned from that what it was all about" (*SR*, 148).

Jake's unfortunate wound has made life for him scarcely more than bearable. The wound from the war has kept him and Brett from becoming true lovers; now Brett moves desperately from one man to another in a futile attempt to resolve her frustration; and Jake tries to combat his feelings of futility through an immersion into the life of the senses—either by way of drink or by way of an occasional fishing trip with his friend Bill Gorton. Even Jake's concept of morality has become in part a matter of sensation—what is moral is what makes you feel good afterwards (*SR*, 149).

Barnes is like his Paris friends in appearance only. While they seem relatively content to perpetuate the rather pointless and careless pattern of their lives, Jake evinces disgust with the physical and emotional excesses around him and more and more draws himself inward and apart from his floundering companions. It is just such an individualistic stance that attracts him so strongly to the young Romero, whose self-sufficiency and protective reserve reinforce his own movement in this direction.

Just as the first half of *The Sun Also Rises* documents further the life the hero rejects, the expatriate's excursion into Spain in the second half of this book can be viewed as emblematic of his search for ethical standards to replace those undermined by war and philistinism at home. Leslie Fiedler tells us that "like the American East, Paris in Hemingway's book stands for the world of women and work, for 'civilization' with all its moral complexity." [4] Just as the hero has rejected the orthodox moral and religious views and emotional complications of "Soldier's Home," he now turns from the irresponsibility and moral defeatism of his Paris friends to what Fiedler refers to as the "simple and joyous anti-civilization" of Spain.

In the trout stream of Burguete, Jake undergoes a kind of regeneration rite similar to that in "Big Two-Hearted River." Yet, despite its obvious therapeutic value, the fishing provides only a momentary diversion—a temporary escape from despair. In order to truly regain his equilibrium, he must find a moral code that he can follow—a belief in certain rules of conduct by which he may acquire the discipline of control and perseverance. Neither books nor religion nor reason has been able to supply him with such a belief. He needs the practical example of men who adhere so strongly to such rules that they are willing to die as well as live by them.

As shown in chapter one, Hemingway had begun to demonstrate his Spanish sensibilities as early as 1924 by contrasting the sterile and impotent image of the Anglo-Saxon world of *In Our Time* with highly sympathetic portraits of matadors interspersed between the stories. In one of these portraits, entitled "The Undefeated," the author introduces not another embodiment of the passive hero, but a man who will teach the hero how to live in a world of death and destruction—who will pass on to him the necessary rules for survival.

The world of Manuel Garcia is no less violent and cruel than that of Nick Adams. A series of unfortunate circumstances has made it necessary for the once prominent bullfighter to beg for work and to hire on in a bullfight in which conditions are overwhelmingly against him. He must fight dangerous, second-rate bulls for pay that will not allow him to engage skilled assistants. A friend warns him against fighting so soon after getting out of the hospital. "You ought to get out and stay out," he says. "Why don't you cut off your coleta, Manolo?" Manuel answers: "I've tried keeping away from it . . . I can't do it. Besides I've been going good lately . . . I got to stick with it, Manos" (*SS*, 243).

The old matador's great sense of pride compels him to stick to his trade and to make the best of a bad situation. "If I can fix it so that I get an even break," he tells his friend, "that's all I want" (*SS*, 243). He reminds his friend of his skill: "You know when I get going I'm good." And when his agent remarks that "There aren't any bullfighters any more," Manolo is quick to assert that "I'm a bullfighter" (*SS*, 236).

As Hemingway would demonstrate many times over from this point on, the bullfighter's simple and unmitigated pride—pride in

his professional skill and in his manly courage—provided at least
one positive standard by which an individual might gain honor
and dignity in a world where those essentials seemed lacking.
Manuel is a simple, primitive man whose courage and integrity
are incorruptible. It is a matter of great professional honor to him
to handle the cape with maximum knowledge and skill, and to
increase the danger to himself by working as close to the bull
as possible. The author says about him:

> He thought in bull-fight terms. Sometimes he had a thought and
> the particular piece of slang would not come into his mind and he
> could not realize the thought. His instincts and his knowledge
> worked automatically, and his brain worked slowly and in words.
> He knew all about bulls. He did not have to think about them. He
> just did the right thing. His eyes noted things and his body
> performed the necessary measures without thought. If he thought
> about it, he would be gone. (*SS*, 260)

Manuel knows that there are tricks by which he might make
the danger to himself appear greater while actually diminishing
the chances of a goring, but his unflinching integrity demands that
he adhere strictly to the rules of the *corrida*. In the bullring, there
is a right way and a wrong way to do things; hence, when Manuel
sizes up his bull for the kill, he knows exactly what it is he must
do.

> Now, facing the bull, he was conscious of many things at the
> same time. There were the horns, the one splintered, the other
> smoothly sharp, the need to profile himself toward the left horn,
> lance himself short and straight, lower the muleta so the bull
> would follow it, and going in over the horns, put the sword all the
> way into a little spot about as big as a five-peseta piece straight
> in the back of the neck, between the pitch of the bull's shoulders.
> He must do all this and must then come out from between the
> horns. He was conscious he must do all this, but his only thought
> was in words: "Corto y derecho." (*SS*, 260)

Manuel discovers, however, that the bull he must kill is not
particularly brave and that consequently he must take increased
risks in order to kill him in a manner that satisfies his sense of
form. "There was nothing to do but go in," he thinks.

> Corto y derecho. He profiled close to the bull, crossed the muleta
> in front of his body and charged. As he pushed in the sword, he
> jerked his body to the left to clear the horn. The bull passed him
> and the sword shot up in the air, twinkling under the arc-lights, to
> fall red-hilted on the sand. (SS, 262)

Again and again Manuel is unsuccessful in his attempt to kill the
bull correctly. Finally, in a mounting rage, with the crowd becoming
increasingly hostile, Manuel thinks to himself: "He'd show them."
And he does show them in the end, even after being tossed and
gored by the bull. Scarcely able to retain his feet and scorning
help from his aides, he goes in for the kill one last time.

> All right, you bastard! Manuel drew the sword out of the muleta,
> sighted with the same movement and flung himself onto the bull.
> He felt the sword go in all the way. Right up to the guard. Four
> fingers and his thumb into the bull. The blood was hot on his
> knuckles, and he was on top of the bull. (SS, 264)

"All right, you bastards!" he says, in contempt for the crowd.

Exactly what the proud and disdainful figure of Manuel Garcia
meant in terms of Hemingway's future development would not
be made clear until 1932, when in *Death In The Afternoon* he devoted
an entire book to an elaboration of the matador's art and character.
But even as early as 1925 it must have been clear to some readers
that Hemingway had introduced, in the character of Manuel Garcia,
a strikingly new note into his fiction. Here was a far different
sort of hero than Hemingway thus far had been depicting. The
earlier hero was a passive or defensive individual—a victim of
circumstances that forced him either to run or to resign himself
to inevitable defeat. Manuel, on the other hand, is conspicuously
in control of his environment. "His work with the red cloth was
to reduce the bull," the author tells us, in order "to make him
manageable" (SS, 255). It is the frustration and relative helplessness
of the bull that is emphasized here, not that of the hero. It is
Manuel's will that is done. It is Manuel who sizes up his adversary,
who plans how to manipulate him, and finally how to dominate
and kill him. Manuel's superior skill and intelligence, as opposed
to the bull's helplessness, is underscored in the following passage.

> Huh! Manuel said, "Toro!" and leaning back, swung the cape
> forward. Here he comes. He side-stepped, swung the cape in back
> of him, and pivoted, so the bull followed a swirl of cape and then
> was left with nothing, fixed by the pass, dominated by the cape.
> Manuel swung the cape under his muzzle with one hand to show
> the bull was fixed, and walked away. (SS, 253)

Finally, "the bull was on the defensive again," and Manuel "brought around the muleta in a half-circle that pulled the bull to his knees," which, in a sense, has virtually been the position of the hero, himself, in earlier stories.

Certainly Manuel has been just as victimized as Hemingway's previous heroes, but, unlike the others, he is self-possessed to the point of arrogance, courageous to the point of recklessness, and a dominator in every sense; this is the kind of man who wins the infinite respect and admiration of the incapacitated Jake Barnes in the last part of *The Sun Also Rises*. This time it is Pedro Romero who embodies ideals of behavior the earlier heroes have found lacking in the world about them, and to whom Jake Barnes will now look for moral support. In contrast to Jake's disappointment over the rootlessness and emotional instability of his Paris friends, the disorganized foreigner finds hope for a better way of life as he watches the self-contained Romero imposing his will upon the savagely charging bull. Though Jake has been rendered impotent and can never hope to completely regain his losses, he can still appreciate Romero and what he stands for. And what he observes are the character attributes and strict code of conduct that become so pronounced in Hemingway's later work.

Even before he encounters Pedro Romero and Juan Belmonte in the Pamplona ring, Jake has more than just a passing interest in the bullfight; in fact, because of his special knowledge of and excitement over this sport, the gap between himself and his Paris friends is even greater than suspected. Jake is immediately identified as having an affinity with the professional bullfight circle from which his friends are conspicuously excluded. Upon his meeting with Montoya, Romero's manager, Jake reports:

> He always smiled as though bull-fighting were a very special
> secret between the two of us; a rather shocking but really very

deep secret that we knew about. He always smiled as though there
were something . . . that we understood. It would not do to expose
it to people who would not understand. (*SR,* 131)

Then Montoya distinguishes Jake from his friends by remarking
that he alone possesses true *aficion*—meaning passion for the bullfight—and puts his hand on Jake's shoulder as if to acknowledge
officially his acceptance among the enchanted circle of bullfighters
(*SR,* 131). Later Jake explains that Montoya's simple gesture had
certain spiritual implications.

> We often talked about bulls and bull-fighters. I had stopped at the
> Montoya for several years. We never talked for very long at a
> time. It was simply the pleasure of discovering what we each felt.
> Men would come in from distant towns and before they left
> Pamplona stop and talk for a few minutes with Montoya about
> bulls. These men were aficionados. Those who were aficionados
> could always get rooms even when the hotel was full. Montoya
> introduced me to some of them. They were always very polite at
> first, and it amused them very much that I should be an
> American. Somehow it was taken for granted that an American
> could not have aficion. He might simulate it or confuse it with
> excitement, but he could not really have it. When they saw that I
> had aficion, and there was no password, no set questions that
> could bring it out, rather it was a sort of oral spiritual examination
> with the questions always a little on the defensive and never
> apparent, there was this same embarrassed putting the hand on
> the shoulder, or a "Buen hombre." But nearly always there was
> the actual touching. It seemed as though they wanted to touch you
> to make it certain. (*SR,* 132)

It soon becomes apparent that Montoya does not want Jake's
friends around, and, as Jake puts it, "they were simply a little
something shameful between us" (*SR,* 132). And later, when Montoya begins to fear that Jake's crowd will have a corrupting influence
on young Romero, Jake conspires with him to keep them apart.
"Don't give Romero the message," Jake tells Montoya, when his
friends invite the matador out to dinner. "You think so?" asks
Montoya. "Absolutely," Jake replies. Then, as Montoya smiles
approvingly, Jake comments: "They're a fine lot. There's one American woman down here now that collects bull-fighters" (*SR,* 172).

As the Pamplona fiesta progresses and Jake takes his friends to see the performances of Romero and Belmonte in the Pamplona ring, the two matadors provide an image of integrity against which his friends, with the exception of Brett, are measured and found wanting. Against the seriousness and dignity of Romero in and out of the ring, Jake's friends are constantly drunk and bickering among themselves, attacking one another with insults just as the helpless steers are attacked during the choosing of the bulls. When Robert Cohn remarks "It's no life being a steer," Mike says, "Don't you think so? I would have thought you'd loved being a steer, Robert" (SR, 141). Ironically, here the entire group takes on the aspect of the steers—aimless and impotent.

In direct contrast to the herding instinct of Jake's companions— Bill Gorton says at one point, "Don't you ever detach me from the herd, Mike" (SR, 141)—Jake identifies Romero as a man who lives and works alone—in a solitude that seems to augment his individual superiority and personal dignity. When Jake first meets Romero, he describes him as "seeming very far away and dignified," and stresses the fact that he is all alone. And when he leaves the matador's room, he observes, "he was standing, straight and handsome and altogether by himself, alone in the room" (SR, 163). It is this extreme sense of self-worth, of his individual superiority among men, that compels Romero to perform always in accordance with the highest standards of his profession.

Jake establishes Romero's supremacy among men and among bullfighters on the basis of three things that he does better in the ring than anyone else. Jake points out:

> In bull-fighting they speak of the terrain of the bull and the
> terrain of the bull-fighter. As long as a bull-fighter stays in his
> own terrain he is comparatively safe. Each time he enters into the
> terrain of the bull he is in great danger. (SR, 213)

Romero possesses the necessary courage to "calmly and quietly let the horns pass him close each time." Jake explains to Brett how close Romero always works to the bull and points out to her the tricks the other bullfighters use to make it look as though they are working closely.

Romero never made any contortions, always it was straight and pure and natural in line. The others twisted themselves like corkscrews, their elbows raised, and leaned against the flanks of the bull after his horns had passed, to give a faked look of danger. Afterward, all that was faked turned bad and gave an unpleasant feeling. Romero's bull-fighting gave real emotion, because he kept the absolute purity of line in his movements and always quietly and calmly let the horns pass him close each time. He did not have to emphasize their closeness. Brett saw how something that was beautiful done close to the bull was ridiculous if it were done a little way off. I told her how since the death of Joselito all the bull-fighters had been developing a technic that simulated this appearance of danger in order to give a fake emotional feeling, while the bull-fighter was really safe. Romero had the old thing, the holding of his purity of line through the maximum of exposure, while he dominated the bull by making him realize he was unattainable, while he prepared him for the killing. (SR, 167, 168)

Jake pays a crowning tribute to Romero's fearlessness by adding that he could never be frightened, because "he knows too damned much. . . . He knew everything when he started. The others can't ever learn what he was born with" (SR, 168).

A second quality Jake comes to admire in the matador—one closely aligned with courage—is the ability to endure physical hardship quietly and alone. This is the virtue Hemingway extolled in the character of Manuel Garcia, and which he now praises in the account of Juan Belmonte, who is fighting despite the paralyzing pain of a fistula. Though Belmonte is hurt, he must endure the indignity and suffering and thus exercise his courage until the final overwhelming mastery of the pain. "Belmonte's jaw came further out in contempt, and his face turned yellower, and he moved with greater difficulty as the pain increased . . . not hearing anything, only going through the pain" (SR, 214, 215). Belmonte's courage appears all the greater in light of the fact that he is working in front of a hostile crowd who neither understands or appreciates his performance.

Besides the emphasis on courage and endurance as exhibited by Romero and Belmonte, a third quality in Romero's performance is still more important as it bears on the development of the Hemingway hero. For the proud and assertive Romero, it is not enough to simply endure—he must prevail.⁵ And this seems to be the greatest source of attraction for Jake as he witnesses Romero's work. He "imposed conditions." At one point Jake excitedly explains to Brett "how Romero took the bull away from a fallen horse with his cape, and how he held him with the cape and turned him, smoothly and suavely," and how *he* saved *his* bulls for the last "when he wanted them" (SR, 167). It is not just that Romero braves the maximum of exposure to himself, but that "he dominated the bull by making him realize he was unattainable, while he prepared him for the killing" (SR, 168).

As in the case of Manuel Garcia, the dramatic contrast between the inaccessibility, or invulnerability, of this man who controls and manipulates his environment and the relative helplessness of Hemingway's early protagonists is noticeable once again. Romero is especially careful to draw attention to "everything of which he could control the locality" (SR, 216). Romero manipulates his adversary with almost arrogant self-confidence, so proud of his dominance that he accentuates it by smiling, turning his back on the bull, "his hand on his hip, his cape on his arm, and the bull watching his back going away." And Jake observes, "it was so slow and so controlled" (SR, 217), as though he were rocking the bull to sleep. Finally, Jake experiences a definite feeling of elation when Romero "killed not as he had been forced to by the last bull, but as he wanted to" (SR, 220).

Most of the characters in *The Sun Also Rises* do not profit by the exhibition of integrity nor do they even recognize it, except for Jake and Brett. Brett is the only one of Jake's crowd who becomes seriously involved in the meaning of the bullfight, just as she is the only one to experience a degree of moral growth through her relationship with Romero. Brett, alone, becomes "absorbed in the professional details" (SR, 211). When Jake asks her to concentrate on the way the bull uses his horns, Brett responds enthusiastically, "I saw it . . . I saw him shift from his left to his right horn," and Jake acknowledges, "Damn good!" (SR, 140) Later on, Brett picks up a bit of information about bullfight conditions that only an *aficionado* would be sensitive to. Just before Romero is to enter the ring, she remarks to Jake, "I'm not worried about him . . . I wish the wind would drop, though" (*SR*, 208). And at the last, when Brett breaks off her relationship with Romero because she knows she will ruin him, she, too, has become affected by Romero's demonstration of proper conduct in and out of the ring. "You know," she says to Jake, "I feel rather damned good . . . it makes one feel rather good deciding not to be a bitch . . . it's sort of what we have instead of God" (*SR*, 245).

Despite Jake's knowledge that there is to be no happy end for Brett and himself, he seems to have at least become aware of a way of living that will impose some meaning and form upon the disorder of his life. The matador's fidelity to a strict code of conduct presents to him a way of achieving honor and dignity even in the face of physical defeat and, possibly, creates in him a willingness to endure despite the terrible odds that are against him.

That Hemingway probably wrote about the emergence of his own passionate interest in the bullfight through the character of Jake Barnes is supported not only by the usual connection between Hemingway and his fictional heroes, the detailed account by Carlos Baker of Hemingway's early years in Spain, and the corroboration of Hadley, but by revealing remarks by two Spanish critics who have been especially sensitive to Spain's influence on Hemingway. Salvador de Madariaga observes that Hemingway "developed roots in Iberian soil," that he was "inside Spain, living her life," and that he may "well have been the non-Spaniard who of all time has come closest to penetrating to her soul." [6] "The start of Hemingway's aficion goes back to the outset of his career," he says, "when as a Paris-based correspondent of the *Toronto Star* he paid a number of visits to Vigo, Pamplona and Mallorca." And he adds, "Spain remained a major source of inspiration to Hemingway during the later twenties while he was achieving fame and developing a characteristic philosophy."

Castillo-Puche was impressed as well by the significant timing of Hemingway's initial attraction to Spain and to the bullfight—that it came just as the author was looking for a ruling philosophy of life and just as he was formulating the essential principles of his craft. "From his very first *corrida* that he saw as a mere reporter," he remarks, "it was to remain in him fixed and indelible, the basis of his elemental philosophy which he would carry with him throughout his life." [7] "From the very first moment," Castillo-Puche points out, "Ernest tended to see in the matador a superhuman power that was more than religious—something almost divine," a power capable of successfully combating in a symbolic way the brute forces of nature. Castillo-Puche stresses particularly the immediate transcendental value of the bullfight for Hemingway, though, at first, as with Jake Barnes, it is grasped only intuitively—in "a powerful intuition which enabled him to penetrate to the ultimate mystery and ritualistic essence of the *corrida*." [8] "The tendidos, barreras, callejon—these were to him a revelation of a metaphysical order," which from the very beginning he was fervently dedicated to deciphering.

Both Spanish commentators agree that in 1932 the meaning of this philosophy and its impact on Hemingway's future work became clear. About *Death In The Afternoon*, Madariaga says, "This is the great book of the bullfight; also of the values Hemingway was learning in Spain." [9] Castillo-Puche observes that, after the author's initial emotional reaction to the *corrida* had been recorded, he set about "dedicating himself objectively, even stubbornly, to experiencing further and documenting the study of our brave and savage fiesta . . . the liturgy of life and death symbolized in the bullfight." [10] At this point Hemingway becomes more than a mere *aficionado*, Castillo-Puche says, "even more than a passionate *aficionado*." [11] His study does much more, he notes, than merely provide artistic commentaries about this or that famous bullfighter, or make apologies for what is accidental and brutal about the bullfight. Rather, his best pages illuminate "the transcendence of our national pastime," and sweep aside for all time the false lyricism and hollow rhetoric "of our so-called journalists of the bullfight." He concludes: "This study about the bullfight will be indispensable for those who wish to study it in a serious way . . . and if only because of this I believe he should receive full respect from all of those who live by the bullfight, the bullfighters and the fiesta." [12]

The next chapter, then, seeks to uncover more about the values implicit in the characters of Manuel Garcia, Juan Belmonte, and Pedro Romero—figures who seem to serve as exemplars of conduct, the embodiment of something better than giving in to futility and submission in the face of adversity—for Hemingway's next four major protagonists. The next chapter also discloses more about the source and meaning of Jake Barnes' "disturbed emotional feeling that always comes after a bullfight, and that feeling of elation that comes after a good bullfight" (SR, 164). Jake's limited attempt to explain the meaning of the bullfight as "something that was going on with a definite end," and as "less of a spectacle with unexplained horrors" (SR, 167) is scarcely adequate in explaining the strength of the appeal the *corrida* has for him.

4 / The Spirit of *Particularismo:* Hemingway's Apotheosis of the Matador in *Death in the Afternoon*

IF THERE is a single thesis to Hemingway's treatise on the bullfight, *Death In The Afternoon,* it might be formulated in these words: this is life, and this is the way to live in it. The world of Nick Adams, Frederick Henry, and Jake Barnes and the Spanish world of *Death In The Afternoon* are the same. Violence, suffering, and death are the rule; only, instead of another fictional projection of Hemingway, it is the author himself who takes the reader on tour through the world of the bullfight, expounding as he goes on the world's injustice and on the Spaniard's fatalistic philosophy of life.

Hemingway says that death and mutilation are just as prevalent in the Spanish world as elsewhere. They turn on you here to kill and break you as surely as they had turned on Henry and Catherine in *A Farewell To Arms.* In one place he describes the tragic end of a young torero who falls prey to the deceit and cruelty of life. He laments that the matador was killed before he ever got going.

> He was twenty years old when he was killed by a Veragua bull that lifted him once, then tossed him against the wood of the foot of the barrera and never left him until the horn had broken up the skull as it might break a flower pot. He was a fine looking boy who had studied the violin until he was fourteen, studied bullfighting until he was seventeen, and fought bulls until he was twenty. They really worshipped him in Valencia and he was killed before they ever had time to turn on him. (*DA,* 45)

57

Almost as if he is echoing the sentiments of Frederick Henry, who had remarked that the very good and the very gentle and the very brave were the first to be killed (*FA*, 259), Hemingway observes here that the most sincere and dedicated matadors are killed more frequently than others. "Granero was the soundest, the healthiest, and the bravest and he was killed in Madrid in the May following the death of Joselito" (*DA*, 104).

Evidently, nothing has happened in the years since the writing of *A Farewell To Arms* to change the author's belief that man's chances for survival are shaped largely by forces beyond his control. In fact, in writing that there are no happy endings in life, he seems to have become more convinced than ever that life is necessarily tragic; he teaches in *Death In The Afternoon* the grim lesson that "our bodies all wear out in some way and we die" (*DA*, 10, 11), and that consequently "no man can escape death by honest effort" (*DA*, 10, 11). "All stories if continued far enough end in death," he says (*DA*, 122). "There is no remedy for anything in life. Death is the sovereign remedy for all misfortunes" (*DA*, 104).

Though Hemingway's outlook on life seems as grave as ever at this point in his career, he appears to have found in the world of his Spanish friends an attitude, or rather a group of attitudes amounting to an ideology, which becomes the prime mover in his approach to life and art. First of all, he seems to have found immense comfort in the fact that the Spanish populace as a whole took suffering and death to be a daily part of their lives and activities. He says:

> They know death is the unescapable reality, the one thing man may be sure of; the only security; that it transcends all modern comforts and that with it you do not need a bathtub in every American home, nor, when you have it, do you need the radio. They think a great deal about death and when they have a religion they have one which believes that life is much shorter than death. (*DA*, 104)

Because of his own obsessive interest in suffering and dying, Hemingway assumed the Spaniard's conclusion that suffering and torment and death are the sum total of life to be a valid one, an accurate assessment of the human condition. He found it especially admirable that the Spanish not only acquiesced to a world of death and violence but that they tried to come into direct contact with it as often as possible in the ritual of the bullfight.

> They take an intelligent interest in death and when they can see it being given, avoided, refused and accepted . . . they pay their money and go to the bullring, continuing to go even when . . . they are most artistically disappointed and emotionally defrauded. (*DA*, 266)

Exactly what the value is in seeing death "being given, avoided, refused and accepted" in the bullring Hemingway is very clear about. "What gave it [the bullfight] continued importance in a barren country like Spain," the author reports,

> . . . was that it kept before men's attention their struggle with the brute forces of nature, to control them to their own ends, in which their human ingenuity gave them the assumption of victory, if they spent their best effort. (*DA*, 189)

Hemingway seemed to sense that, in what appeared to him to be a symbolic life-and-death struggle of the bullring, he had found an antidote to the feeling of inner helplessness experienced by Frederick Henry and Nick Adams and Jake Barnes. The bullfight could be viewed as a microcosm of man eternally pitting himself against the destructive forces of nature and the overwhelming odds of death, but with one very important difference. In the bullring, the forces of death are not nebulous and impersonal, but rather are reduced to something that can be grasped and reacted against. Within the classical form of the *corrida*, one's adversary is given shape and purpose, and the strict requirements of the fight give man the chance to focus and discharge his pent-up aggressions on the object of the bull. The presence of a definite, threatening enemy whom it is possible to hate and to combat on even or, perhaps, better than even terms, provides not only this opportunity for cathartic release but for at least a temporary, if illusory, victory over death.

Even death itself becomes bearable, even meaningful, within the ritualized purposes of the bullfight. If the matador dies, he has the chance to die nobly, fighting bravely and with integrity. Pain and mutilation are also justified, because one understands that they are a necessary part of the symbolic life-and-death struggle. "I believe that the tragedy of the bullfight is so well ordered and so strongly disciplined by ritual," Hemingway says, "that a person feeling the whole tragedy cannot separate the minor comic-tragedy of the horse so as to feel it emotionally" (*DA*, 8). Hemingway believes that anyone having this sense of the tragedy and ritual of the fight should be reconciled to the minor aspects, such as the pain suffered by the horses, since it is only important as it relates to the whole. In a vein that seems more hopeful than convincing, Hemingway says "After a while you never notice anything disgusting" (*DA*, 8). This is precisely what Jake Barnes (withdrawing behind the protective shield of ritual) says to Brett when she wonders how she will hold up during her first bullfight. "Just don't watch when it's bad," he says (*SR*, 162) [1] And later,

> I sat beside Brett and explained to Brett what it was all about. I told her about watching the bull, not the horse, when the bulls charged the picadors, and got her to watching the picador place the point of his pic so that she saw what it was all about, so that it became more something that was going on with a definite end, and less a spectacle with unexplained horrors. (*SR*, 167)

This partially explains that disturbed emotional feeling that Jake Barnes always experienced after a bullfight. Hemingway tells us in *Death In The Afternoon* about his own feeling of elation after a good bullfight, "I feel very fine while it is going on and have a feeling of life and death and mortality and immortality, and after it is all over I feel very sad but very fine" (*DA*, 2). But ultimately the source of this feeling can be identified much more definitively.

Far more fascinating to Hemingway than the Spaniard's acceptance of the reality of death was his manner of facing it. What the Spaniard mainly went to see in the course of the bullfight Hemingway describes as "the feeling of rebellion against death which comes from its administering" (*DA*, 233). Because the Spaniard is a man in rebellion against death, the author informs us:

He has pleasure in taking to himself one of the Godlike attributes; that of giving it. This is one of the most profound feelings in those men who enjoy killing. These things are done in pride and pride, of course, is a Christian sin, and a pagan virtue. But it is pride which makes the bullfight and true enjoyment of killing which makes the great matador. (*DA*, 233) [2]

Here is the chief motivating force in the character of the matador—this strained spirit of rebellion and prideful individualism—that both Jake Barnes and Ernest Hemingway found so attractive. Speaking of the matador's seemingly heroic attitude of resistance to authority and domination—his chin-protruding defiance of death in the bullring—Hemingway says that *pundonor*, with pride as its governing virtue, is the strongest characteristic of the Spanish race; and the ideals which make up *pundonor*—pride, dignity, courage, defiance, and honor—are those that guide the matador in the bullring. These ideals, Hemingway notes, are not those which caused Frederick Henry's embarrassment. They still have concreteness for the Spaniard: honor, courage, and glory "may be as real a thing as water, wine or olive oil" (*DA*, 92).

Hemingway's view of the Spaniard as a rebellious and defiant individual seems to be borne out by other interpreters of Spanish character. According to Angel Ganivet, for instance, the inflexible framework upon which the Spanish moral character rests is that of almost belligerent independence, which is actually a philosophy of life. Ganivet points out that to speak of this moral element in the personality of the Spaniard is to speak perforce of the moral stoicism of Seneca, which he expresses in these words:

Do not allow anything alien to your spirit to conquer you; in the midst of life's struggles, believe implicitly that you have within you a source of strength, something powerful and indestructible, something like a jeweled shaft about which orbit the wretched happenings of your daily life; and regardless of the events that may involve you, whether they bring prosperity or debasement, remain firm and erect, and then the least we can say of you is that you are a man. [3]

This spirit of independence, which Hemingway found functioning so dramatically in the matador and which he would express later in terms of his last heroes, Ganivet identifies as an ideal that touches

every phase of the Spanish personality and the Spanish national
life. The peninsula wants to be let alone, he says, the province
wants to be let alone, and the individual wants to be let alone.
Ganivet points out that since each province is a separate Spain,
instead of speaking of *España* as a nation, the Spanish portion of
the Iberian peninsula should be referred to as *Las Españas*. And,
significantly, Ganivet explains that this rivalry among provinces
is a result of fear of domination—in this case, by a stronger neigh-
bor.[4] Salvador de Madariaga speaks of this national spirit of independence as follows:

> Within the nation, regional characters stood distinctly separate
> with a mutual differentiation, a mutual assertion of individualism
> which drove inwards, into the very soul of the nation, the vigorous
> individualism wherewith the nation confronted the outside world.[5]

As another example of the pervasive spirit of independence of
the Spaniard, Ganivet points to the guerrilla spirit of the Spanish
soldier, which, at a later point in his career, Hemingway would
point to with reluctance as the reason for the failure of the Spanish
army to fight as a well-coordinated, closely knit unit. Ganivet says,
"Every Spanish military leader, from El Cid and Gonzalo de Cor-
doba to the more recent leaders of Spanish civil strife, has been
a roving king, a warrior, master of his own fate, responsible to
no one, and accepting no dictate save that of his own conscience."[6]

This essentially anarchistic spirit is again evident, according to
Ganivet, in the judicial code of the Spaniard. The ideal of justice
to the Spaniard may be condensed in the following words: "This
Spaniard is authorized to do as he pleases."[7] Thus the Spaniard
goes above the law in judicial matters; he constitutes himself as
judge and jury. And too often he takes direct action in which the
ideas of other individuals or groups are not taken into consideration.
For a Spaniard there is but one solution to a problem—his own
solution. Swept forth by his abhorrence of outside authority, he
is absolutely certain that he holds "THE TRUTH" in the fullness
of its glory and that the "others" cannot fail "to see the light."[8]

This same intense individualism of the Spaniard Ortega y Gasset
calls *particularismo*, which he describes as: "That spiritual state in

which we believe that we don't have the obligation to consider
the opinions or the lives of others."[9] Because of the Spaniard's
particularismo, Ortega says, and the reticence and lack of communication it breeds, the soldier, the individualist, the intellectual,
the farmer, and the worker moves alone, within his own tight
sphere, placidly ignoring others.[10] For this reason, he concludes:

> In our country, living together is always a cause for
> misunderstanding. . . . The Spaniard cannot bring himself to
> abandon his immediate and primary perspective, in which he is
> the focal point and everything else is in a periphery dependent on
> him.[11]

Ortega feels that a perfect embodiment of the Spaniard's contempt for the opinions of others is to be found in his *pronunciamientos*,
which he describes as personal manifestoes in which the individual
proclaims the "truth" as he sees it and, as he candidly believes,
everyone else sees it. It is not necessary to struggle to convince
his fellow men. They already think the same way. All that is
necessary is to "declare" the truth publicly and the masses will
respond and the battle will be won without firing a shot.[12]

Ultimately, Ortega underscores Hemingway's thesis that the
reason for the obstinacy of the Spaniard—for his aversion to authority and domination—is found in his congenital sense of pride, the
inbred aristocracy that raises the peasant to the level of the king
and his courtiers, and demands the inalienable rights of the Spaniard from anyone who may attempt to exert an arrogant and en-
croaching authority. This spirit of revolt, this cry for independence,
is explained also by Allison Peers in his book called *Spain:*

> We who are as good as you, swear to you who are no better than
> we, to accept you as our King and sovereign lord, provided you
> observe all our statutes and laws; and if not, no (Si no, no).[13]

This prideful guardianship by the Spaniard of his innate aristocracy
intrigued James Russell Lowell during his visit in Spain and led
him to remark in his book *Impressions Of Spain:*

> Every Spaniard is a caballero, and every Spaniard can rise from
> the ranks to position and power. . . . Manners, as in France, are

democratic and the ancient nobility here as a class are even more shadowy than the dwellers in the Faubourg St. Germain.[14]

This Spanish rebellion against authority, which springs from the Spaniard's exalted sense of pride, Hemingway found manifested in the defiant pose of the matador. This same individualism, seen in other phases of the Spanish life, is found in its purest form in the art of the matador. Here is a man, Hemingway found, whose tough shell of individualism nothing can possibly penetrate. No matter how adverse the conditions in which he finds himself working, he has his sense of *pundonor* to keep him firm, erect, and unyielding, and to propel him toward goals of supreme perfection.

Hemingway's description of Manuel Maera's last tragic season as a bullfighter, depicted in *Death In The Afternoon*, displays all the essential virtues of the author's previous matador heroes. "He was the proudest man I have ever seen," Hemingway says. "He had a complete knowledge of bulls and a valor that was absolute and a solid part of him. When the bulls did not come to him he did not point out the fact to the crowd asking for their indulgence and sympathy, he went to the bulls, arrogant, dominating, and disregarding danger" (*DA*, 79). Maera exhibits the same reckless stance before death and brings the same rebellious attitudes to his work as Hemingway's future heroes, Harry Morgan, Colonel Cantwell, Robert Jordan, and Santiago.

Maera's last season in the ring is a monument to both his courage and his arrogant indomitability. Hemingway writes:

> But all the last year he fought you could see he was going to die. He had galloping consumption and he expected to die before the year was out. In the meantime he was very occupied. He was gored badly twice but he paid no attention to it. It hurt as a torn wound made by a splintered horn hurts after two days but he paid no attention to the pain. He acted as though it were not there. He did not favor it or avoid lifting the arm; he ignored it. He was a long way beyond pain. I never saw a man to whom time seemed so short as it did to him that season. The next time I saw him he had been gored in the neck in Barcelona. The wound was closed with eight stitches and he was fighting, his neck bandaged, the day after. His neck was stiff and he was furious at the

stiffness he could do nothing about and the fact that he had to
wear a bandage that showed above his collar. *(DA, 91)*

In addition to this conspicuous display of fortitude, Maera gains
heroic stature by deliberately provoking danger to himself by his
style of fighting, braving the maximum of danger and then control-
ling that danger in order to demonstrate his complete domination
of his opponent. Because he is "in rebellion against death," he
must attempt to impose his will in a way that will give the most
vivid dramatization of the authority of the individual personality.
In the measure in which this domination is accentuated, Hemingway
claims, will it be beautiful to watch *(DA, 79)*.

The climax of the matador's rebellion in the bullring, Hemingway
says, comes during the brief, last seconds of the fight when the
matador and the bull are both ready for the kill. In the moment
of the final sword thrust, what the matador calls his moment of
truth, the courage and the need to dominate, which demands he
provoke the maximum of danger to himself, show themselves
clearest; because the act is so simple, it is easier to detect the use
of trickery by which the matador might try to lessen the danger
to himself. Thus, in the last fight of Manuel Maera, during his
moment of truth, his honor demands that he kill in a certain way—a
way that will emphasize his courage and ability to dominate. He
has dislocated his wrist killing one time and, despite the pain,
goes in for the kill time and again.

> He lifted the sword with his right hand and the wrist would not
> hold it and it dropped. He lifted the wrist and bended it against
> his doubled left fist, then picked up the sword in his left hand,
> placed it in his right and as he held it you could see the sweat run
> down his face. . . . Now at any time he could have without danger
> or pain slipped the sword into the neck of the bull, let it go into
> the lung or out the jugular and killed him with no trouble. But his
> honor demanded that he kill him high up between the shoulders
> going in as a man should, over the horn, following the sword with
> his body. And on the sixth time he went in this way and the
> sword went in too. He came out from the encounter, the horn just
> clearing his belly as he shrugged over it and as he passed and
> then stood, tall and sunken-eyed, his face wet with sweat, his hair

down on his forehead, watching the bull as he swung, lost his feet
and rolled over. He pulled the sword out with his right hand, as
punishment for it, I suppose, but shifted it to his left, and carrying
it point down, walked over to the barrera. (*DA*, 81)

Actually, the emphasis here on the importance of death expertly
delivered as a source of honor and pride is a value only implicitly
touched on by Hemingway before this. But now he states that
the matador's ability to function as a "skillful killer" is one of
his greatest virtues. A great bullfighter must love to kill, Hemingway
explains sympathetically.

Unless he feels it is the best thing he can do, unless he is
conscious of its dignity and feels it is its own reward, he will be
incapable of the abnegation that is necessary in real killing. The
truly great killer must have a sense of honor and a sense of glory
far beyond that of the ordinary bullfighter. In other words he
must be a simpler man. Also he must take pleasure in it, not
simply as a trick of the wrist, eye, and managing of his left hand
that he does better than other men, which he will naturally have
as a simple man, but he must have a spiritual enjoyment of the
moment of killing. Killing cleanly and in a way which gives you
aesthetic pleasure and pride has always been one of the greatest
enjoyments of a part of the human race. (*DA*, 232)

Don Miguel de Unamuno seems also to have shared Hemingway's
peculiar, perhaps distorted awareness that for the Spaniard killing
in a certain way might serve as a source of value. Speaking of
the "flavor of blood and tragedy" that he found in most aspects
of Spanish life and environment, he remarks:

We really die, and without doubt, we kill completely. We kill the
bull like a good Christian Spaniard in the good old days killed a
dog and an infidel, completely.[15]

What Hemingway the artist learns from the defiant lifestyle
of the matador and the way in which he incorporates this knowledge
into his later fiction, is, of course, central to this thesis. Chapter
five investigates the notion that the author's last four major protagonists demonstrate just those Spanish tendencies Hemingway
apotheosized in the person of the matador, and that, consequently,

they are far different people—more aggressive and defiant—than the author's earlier protagonists. But first, a look at some of his personal attitudes as expressed in *Green Hills Of Africa* will further disclose how profoundly Hemingway was influenced by the personality and craft of the matador at this point in his career.

5 / Hemingway the Matador: His Identification with the Matador's Craft and Code

MANUEL GARCÍA MAERA, who was "generous, humorous, proud, bitter, foulmouthed and a great drinker," prefigured the central character of *Green Hills Of Africa*. Having been deeply moved by the exhibition of manhood of such men as Maera and Pedro Romero, Hemingway seemed bent on sharing the matador's proximity to death and on imposing the same rigid rules of conduct upon his favorite pastime, hunting, and on his trade, writing, as guided the performance of Maera and Romero in the bullring. Apparently he felt that in exhibiting the same reckless stance before death and bringing the same defiant attitudes to his profession as Maera he had found a correct way to live—what Brett called in *The Sun Also Rises* "what we have instead of God."

In *Green Hills Of Africa* Hemingway says he has learned the necessary rules and what precautions to take to "last and get your work done." He has learned to "make it," and now, on this violent hunting expedition to the heart of the African jungle, he attempts to explain these rules and to justify his life and art in terms of the matador's exaltation of daring and artistic integrity. Hemingway explained in *Death In The Afternoon* that the matador's fierce pride demands that he face danger and possible death over and over again to assert his individual superiority as an artist, and now Hemingway transfers the bullfighter's values to his own art in setting up terms for greatness.[1]

In *Death In The Afternoon*, already exploiting the kinship between bullfighting and writing, Hemingway had written that his guiding rule as a writer was never to write a false line (*DA*, 54). "If a man writes clearly enough," he declares, "anyone can see if he fakes" (*DA*, 53). About the book called *Virgin Spain*, Hemingway said, "the result was the unavoidable mysticism of a man who writes a language so badly he cannot make a clear statement, complicated by whatever pseudo-scientific jargon is in style at the moment" (*DA*, 53). Hemingway's pride as a writer compelled him to look now at fellow writers as one matador looked at his rival on a Sunday afternoon: competitively (*GHA*, 198).[2] From now on he sizes up his opponents as the matador sizes up his bull, determining what he has to beat in order to retain his ranking as torero número uno.

In *Green Hills Of Africa* Hemingway is particularly contemptuous of writers with low standards whose effects are achieved through fakery and with tricks. Convinced now of the need for uncompromising standards in a world that preys on the unwary, he speaks of the writer's need for an "absolute conscience . . . to prevent faking" (*GHA*, 23). Like the matador, Hemingway feels that facing his performance as a creative artist each day presents a new challenge to his artistic integrity and to his technical skill, and he asserts that only that writing which is done "without tricks and without cheating" will not "go bad afterwards" (*GHA*, 22). In *The Sun Also Rises*, Jake had said about those bullfighters who used tricks to "give a faked look of danger" that "afterward, all that was faked turned bad and gave an unpleasant feeling" (*SR*, 168).

What the bullfighter accomplishes with the sword and muleta becomes the corollary of what Hemingway wishes to accomplish with words. In connection with the bullfighter's integrity is identified Hemingway's determined effort to be emotionally honest, to render the emotions pure, straight, and unfaked.[3] And the bullfighter's discipline and integrity and skill in handling violence in the ring becomes a paradigm for Hemingway's being able to write well about what he sees—"knowing truly what you really felt, rather than what you were supposed to feel," and putting "down what really happened in action. . . .the real thing, the sequence of motion and fact which made the emotion and which would be as valid in a year or in ten years or with luck and if you stated it purely enough, always . . ." (*DA*, 2).

Just as the matador must brave the maximum of exposure to demonstrate his artistic skill and integrity, Hemingway now suggests that his own greatness as a writer is only possible insofar as he braves physical danger and possible destruction in order to express exactly what happened in action—particularly violent action. His pride as an artist will allow him, he states, to write only of what he has actually felt and seen, using his body as a testing ground for experience (*DA*, 278).[4]

In *Green Hills Of Africa*, Hemingway shows, in, perhaps, a strained effort to identify himself as closely as possible with the matador, that in many respects writing is to be considered as dangerous a profession as bullfighting. "Above all," he says about the writer, "he must survive" (*GHA*, 23). "The hardest thing, because time is so short, is for him to survive and get his work done" (*GHA*, 23). Just as the matador must understand and learn to control such variables of circumstance as the wind, the nature of his bull, the nature of the terrain, his own nerves, and so forth, Hemingway claims that it is almost impossible—though necessary—for a person to "come through all the influences that press on a writer" (*GHA*, 23).

Writers are destroyed in many ways, he says:

> First, economically. They make more money. It is only by hazard that a writer makes money although good books always make money eventually. Then our writers when they have some money increase their standard of living and they are caught. They have to write to keep up their establishments, their wives, and so on, and they write slop. It is slop not on purpose but because it is hurried. Because they write when there is nothing to say or no water in the well. Because they are ambitious. Then, once they have betrayed themselves, they justify it and you get more slop. Or else they read the critics. If they believe the critics when they say they are great then they must believe them when they say they are rotten and they lose confidence. . . . The women writers become Joan of Arc without the fighting. They become leaders. It doesn't matter who they lead. If they do not have followers they invent them. . . . The others try to save their souls with what they write. . . .

> Others are ruined by the first money, the first praise, the first at-
> tack, the first time they cannot write, or the first time they cannot
> do anything else, or else they get frightened and join organizations
> that do their thinking for them. (*GHA*, 20, 21)

These are the things that may ruin a writer before his time; other
hazards Hemingway lumps together into "Politics, women, drink,
money, ambition," and "the lack of politics, women, drink, money,
and ambition" (*GHA*, 23). A few years later, Hemingway would
dramatically illustrate, through the characters of Francis Macomber
and Harry, the dying writer in "The Snows Of Kilimanjaro," the
threat of women and money to a writer's integrity. Both men have
lost what was once most dear to them—liberty and integrity, which
they have traded for security and comfort. Significantly enough,
Francis Macomber manages to regain his moral manhood by assuming the aggressive stance of the torero. Just as the matador
proves his integrity and courage in the bullring by defying the
onrushing bull, Francis Macomber kneels in the path of the oncom-
ing buffalo and thus attains a kind of fearless self-trust and happiness he has never known before. He achieves a moral rebirth by
acting bravely during his supreme moment of truth.

In *Green Hills Of Africa*, the results of Hemingway's *particularismo*
are everywhere in evidence. His deference to and humility before
his fellow writers has disappeared. In its place appears the penchant
for issuing *pronunciamientos*, personal manifestoes in which he proclaims the "truth" as he sees it and, as he candidly believes, everyone else sees it. As noted in chapter three, the Spaniard does not
believe it is necessary to struggle to convince his fellow men. All
that is necessary is "to declare" the truth publicly and the masses
will respond and the battle will be won without firing a shot. Now
Hemingway offers such "declarations," overloaded with presump-
tion, in the form of severe indictments of all those who do not
share his particular artistic tendencies.

From this perspective, Hemingway even manages to turn his
own traumatic war experiences into something absolutely essential
to the writer, contending that, since it was a vital part of his
education as man and artist, no writer should be without it.

I thought about Tolstoi and about what a great advantage an
experience of war was to a writer. It was one of the major subjects
and certainly one of the hardest to write truly of and those writers
who had not seen it were always jealous and tried to make it
seem unimportant, or abnormal, or a disease as a subject, while,
really, it was just something quite irreplaceable they had missed.
(*GHA*, 50)

Frederick Henry's despair was mainly over the horrible sense of
injustice he felt, but now Hemingway is able to state:

Writers are forged in injustice as a sword is forged. . . . Stendhal
had seen a war and Napoleon taught him to write. . . . Dostoevsky
was made by being sent to Siberia. . . . I wondered if it would
make a writer of him, give him the necessary shock to cut the
overflow of words and give him a sense of proportion, if they sent
Tom Wolfe to Siberia or to the Dry Tortugas. (*GHA*, 51)

Hemingway's personal image of himself as man and writer becomes something he promotes at every opportunity, and especially
notable is a good deal of strained animosity for fellow writers.[5]
His anecdote about Scott Fitzgerald in "The Snows of Kilimanjaro"
has been called the public burial of Hemingway's long time friend,
and Fitzgerald was deeply offended. Hemingway deleted the refer-
ence to Scott in the anthologized version, but the original has
Hemingway's writer hero musing on his own life among the American rich. 'He remembered poor Scott, and his romantic awe of
them and how he had started a story once that began, 'The very
rich are different from you and me!' And how someone had said
to Scott, 'Yes, they have money.' " The anecdote concludes, "He
thought they were a special glamorous race, and when he found
they weren't, it wrecked him just as much as any other thing
wrecked him." [6]

In an article entitled "You Could Always Come Back," Maxwell
Geismar associates Hemingway's failures in *Green Hills Of Africa*,
i.e., "the braggadocio, the rather sophomoric, sophisticated smart-
ness . . . the mannerisms, . . ." with the author's consuming passion
for bullfighting and his idealization of the matador. "Hemingway
protests rather too constantly the significance of his achievement,
and his own pleasure, and the ignorance of those who would doubt

his importance and pleasure. And there is misplaced irritation which runs through the book, of which we never seem to find the true object; all the unhappy evidences of a morality which is disputing, by all sorts of indirection, its own moral values." [7]

The epitome of this "unhappy evidence" of a suspect morality comes most alarmingly in the form of Hemingway's "ecstatic adulation" over killing and dominating that Max Eastman spoke of in his article "Bull In The Afternoon." [8] Now that Hemingway the writer-matador has been observed asserting himself as creative artist, establishing the norms and standards for writing that he deems necessary "to survive and get his work done," look for a moment at Hemingway the killer-matador, who derives both emotional and esthetic pleasure and pride from killing cleanly and well, drawing his rifle sights on a buck and dispatching it with an accuracy and released tension that approximates the final sword thrust of the torero. This is what the other half of *Green Hills Of Africa* is about, Hemingway the matador in active rebellion against death, in pursuit of the huge beautiful kudu bull or, more to the point, immortality.

Hemingway's affinity with the bullfighter, especially with Manuel García Maera, who was "proud, bitter, foulmouthed and a great drinker," who "neither sucked after intellectuals nor married money," is shown by the striking similarity in their attitudes toward killing. Both are disturbingly self-engrossed in the sense of glory the matador derives from killing with emotional and artistic integrity. Both, according to Hemingway, are great killers because they "love to kill," and because they believe that killing is its own reward.

Hemingway's interrogator in *Green Hills Of Africa* is bewildered to find that the author derives as much pleasure from hunting kudu as he does from writing well. "One is as necessary as the other," he tells him (*GHA*, 21). One is as necessary as the other because both provide the sense of rebellion, of defiance, that Hemingway saw demonstrated in the bullring and which he now draws on as a major source of inspiration for work as well as for life. Both provide a sense of power and pride if executed with skill and courage.

That Hemingway functions in accordance with the matador's ethics is indicated when he says that dealing out death yields pleasure only insofar as it is done courageously and cleanly—"that I would only shoot as long as I could kill cleanly and as soon as I lost that ability I would stop" (*GHA*, 21). This is reminiscent of his praise of the bullfighter who, when he is no longer capable of performing well, either through old age or fear, leaves his profession.

> Bullfighting is the only art in which the artist is in danger of death and in which the degree of brilliance in the performance is left to the fighter's honor. . . . Once his honor is gone and he finds that he no longer can do great work even when he has a good bull and makes the great effort to nerve himself . . . the next year is usually the one in which he retires. Because a Spaniard must have some honor and when he no longer has the honor-among-thieves sort of belief that he can be good if he only wants to as sustenance then he retires and he gains honor for that decision. (*DA*, 91, 92)

In Hemingway's execution of the kudu, his chief sense of triumph comes from adhering to the strict requirements of the bullfight—from killing well, with honor. After making an extremely difficult and hazardous shot on a rhino, the author fills with elation and knows he will savor the emotion for a long time to come. "Don't worry about how I feel about it," he tells his guide, "I can wake up and think about that any night" (*GHA*, 57). But later in the book his failure to kill well, when he gets his chance at the sable bull he has been pursuing, fills him with dread.

> But it was excited shooting, all of it, and I was not proud of it. I had gotten excited and shot at the whole animal instead of the right place and I was ashamed. (*GHA*, 175)

Like the matador, Hemingway now has an obsessive notion of how things should be done, and his *particularismo* leads him to construct melodramatic contrasts between good and bad writing, good and bad people, and good and bad killings; *Green Hills Of Africa* is built on such contrasts, and underlining every passage is Hemingway's Spanish pride in displaying his own masculine skill and courage. So intent is Hemingway in carrying out his masquerade as a matador that the enactment of his "performance en route to death," with clenched teeth and sucked-in belly, verges on caricature. Emotions seem strained and self-induced, and violence exhibited for its own sake.

One final example portrays Hemingway as the matador-killer, whose pride in doing things the Spanish way, within the rules of the stylized code of conduct he has set up for himself, shows again his spiritual affinity with the matador. The following passage is comparable to the description of Maera, on page 65 killing his last bull, "whose honor demanded that he kill him high up between the shoulders, going in as a man should, over the horn, following the sword with his body." Hemingway, in turn, describes the bull he must kill as having to put his head down to hook, "like any bull, and that will uncover the old place the boys wet their knuckles on and I will get one in there and then must go sideways into the grass," just as Maera shrugs over the horn after the kill. And just as Maera will not settle for anything less than a perfect kill, Hemingway "shot for his neck, slowly and carefully, missing him eight times straight in a mounting, stubborn rage . . . shooting exactly for the same place in the same way each time . . . determined to break his neck" (*GHA,* 58). Later, when Hemingway shows displeasure over not having bagged the largest bull, his guide reminds him of what is most important anyway. "You can always remember how you shot them," he says. "That's what you really get out of it." (*GHA,* 197) Patting Hemingway on the back the guide says, "You god damned bull-fighter" (*GHA,* 196). In Hemingway's eyes, this was probably the highest tribute that could have been accorded him.

It is significant that Hemingway began his next book, *To Have And Have Not* (1937), in Spain, since it is Hemingway's first major exercise in demonstrating the spirit of *pundonor* and *particularismo* exhibited by his later heroes. From this point on, Hemingway's protagonists are, like Harry Morgan, measured by the inflexible standards of behavior upon which the character of the Spanish matador rests. Against the confusion and helplessness of his earlier

protagonists—Nick Adams, Frederick Henry, and Jake Barnes—
Hemingway's last four heroes live in adherence to a strict moral
code that places a premium on stoical courage and perseverance
and fosters an attitude of active rebellion in the face of inevitable
defeat. These men are all faced with the same problems of fear,
violence, and death that produce a state of emotional paralysis
in Hemingway's earlier characters, but the disdainful and recklessly
aggressive manner with which they try to meet them designates,
from their creator's standpoint, their moral superiority.

In tracing the Spanish element in the character of Hemingway's
last heroes, the presence of a new kind of conflict within the mind
of these men is also noticeable—a psychic interplay between the
opposing forces of what might be called compassion and restraint
on the one hand, and aggression and destructive pride on the other.
In the course of this agonized interplay, the force of extreme
individualism and primitive aggression generally holds sway; the
hero's fatalistic acceptance of the Spaniard's view of the world as
endlessly unjust and destructive leads him to sanction the destructive impulse to cruelty and death-dealing in himself and in the
world around him. But at more rational moments, the hero seems
to recognize that these aggressive impulses are preludes to moral
and physical disaster, that they have served only to further brutalize
his spirit and to lead him into fruitless self-laceration and tragic
self-absorption. This agonized coexistence of warring forces in the
minds of Harry Morgan, Colonel Cantwell, Robert Jordan, and
Santiago might be pointed to as the source of their common tragedy.
The spirit of each man is dualistic and polarized; each, to use a
limited metaphor, has within him a kind of Don Quixote and
Sancho Panza. And the struggle of each of these men to reconcile
these contradictory forces creates the powerful source of tension
within their characters. Ultimately, the most convincing heroes are
those in whom the attitudes of *particularismo* and *pundonor* are most
effectively combatted, while those like Harry Morgan and Colonel
Cantwell, who are unrelievedly bellicose and aggressive, are much
more one dimensional.

Hemingway, himself, had experienced such a conflict in the
writing of *Green Hills Of Africa*. At first he seemed thoroughly

committed to the Spaniard's belief that the destructive instinct was both profound and natural, and that "killing is its own reward." But then, he is not above experiencing pangs of guilt when he reflects on what it must be like for the animal who is wounded and suffering but not killed.

I thought suddenly how a bull elk must feel if you break a shoulder and he gets away and in that night I lay and felt it all, the whole thing as it would happen from the shock of the bullet to the end of the business and, being a little out of my head, thought perhaps what I was going through was a punishment for all hunters. (GHA, 21)

His uneasiness is only momentary, however, and he quickly legitimizes the dealing out of suffering and death according to the motivation of the matador. Man is both hunter and the hunted; he only gives what he takes, meeting aggression with aggression. And if he gives it with skill and courage, he gains a sense of defiance and pride that climaxes his rebellion against the presiding powers of the universe.

Then, getting well, I decided if it was a punishment I had paid it and at least I knew what I was doing. I did nothing that had not been done to me. I had been shot and I had been crippled and gotten away. I expected always to be killed by one thing or another and I, truly, did not mind that anymore. (GHA, 21)

Later on, the author's conscience again will not let him rest because he has only wounded his prey, gut-shooting him instead of killing him quickly by breaking his neck as he had attempted.

I was thinking about the bull and wishing to God I had never hit him. Now I had wounded him and lost him. . . . Tonight he would die and the hyenas would eat him, or worse, they would get him before he died, hamstringing him and pulling his guts out while he was alive. . . . I felt a son of a bitch to have hit him and not killed him. (GHA, 183)

But, as before, Hemingway is again able to absolve himself from guilt by assuming the Spaniard's "common sense" attitude toward killing and death. He reminds himself that since death is the inevitable climax to things anyway and since the natural devouring

and self-devouring process that goes on nightly will continue with
or without his participation, he might just as well indulge his
primitive appetites as one who takes pleasure in the beauty of
violence and death gracefully administered.

> I did not mind killing anything, any animal, if I killed it cleanly,
> they all had to die and my interference with the nightly and the
> seasonal killing that went on all the time was very minute and I
> had no guilty feeling at all. (GHA, 183)

Significantly enough, Unamuno and other prominent critics of
the Spanish character have observed just such an internal struggle
taking place within the mind and heart of the Spaniard. "The spirit
is dualistic and polarized," says Unamuno. "Don Quixote and
Sancho Panza travel together, they help one another, they love
one another, but they can't unite." [9] According to Unamuno, this
conflictive nature of Spain and of all things Spanish—the contradiction between the will to peace and the will to aggression—is
the single but powerful source of her fundamental tragedy. The
warring coexistence of humanistic ideas, el humanismo, with its
emphasis on peace and love and understanding, along with the
antithetical effects of militant individualism is the primary reason
for the Spaniard's "irrational" way of life, Unamuno tells us.

Unamuno goes on to state that this inner tension, oppressive
and illogical, is the essence of Spain's temperamental soul: angry
voices blended with sane words; fierce cruelty linked with deep
charity, all the confused shreds of the anarchist and absolutist
character.[10] There can be no harmony, he says, in that war which
each Spaniard wages against himself and his antagonists, but only
perpetual strife, interminable contradiction, and continual incivility.
All identity or even harmony of opposites is undone in the perpetual
battle between heart and head. Each feeds on the other and neither
benefits from the struggle. Thus, Unamuno concludes, the Spaniard
who seems to be plain, simple, and straightforward, becomes a
most complex reality seething with confusion and contradiction.[11]

Most noteworthy is the fact that this merger of contradictory
forces seems to account for the apparently paradoxical attitudes

of Hemingway's last four heroes. This split in the hero's personality can actually be traced as far back as *The Sun Also Rises.* Jake Barnes' mental state varies between softness and toughness. One moment he strikes out viciously at Robert Cohn, and the next moment he is polite and considerate, feeling disgusted with himself. Pulled one way by his determination to be hard, he castigates Cohn rigorously, then pulled by feelings of compassion, Cohn is pardoned in order to satisfy Jake's other self. But Jake's *particularismo* is still in its incipient stage; it is the spirit of despair rather than *pundonor* that prevails in Jake's outlook. He can erect a barrier only of stoical acceptance. In the later heroes, Jake's pervasive gloom has been counteracted by the attitudes of *particularismo* and *pundonor*, though the facade of the matador never totally obscures the old despair. As Hemingway's own stirrings of conscience increase over the years in direct proportion to his increasing commitment to *particularismo* and *pundonor*, so the conflict in the mind of the hero becomes more severe, self-conscious, and articulated.[12]

The point made in the remaining chapters is that Harry Morgan, Robert Jordan, Colonel Cantwell, and Santiago share three tendencies that have been identified as peculiarly Spanish. Each shares the Spaniard's tragic view of life; each exhibits the Spaniard's particularist inclinations to rebellion and finite individualism; and each experiences internal strife as a result of the interplay between the will to aggression and rebellion—as epitomized in the ritual of the bullfight—and the will to peace and human solidarity.[13]

6 / Performance en Route to Death: Part One The Spanish Element in Harry Morgan and Robert Jordan

EDGAR JOHNSON, in discussing the course of Hemingway's career, links the name of Harry Morgan to several matadors Hemingway had apotheosized at an earlier date. "He is the man-against-the-world," Johnson says, "the heroic individual, like the Garcias and Romeros in the daily risking of his life, the pitting of his wits against circumstance." [1] Unlike Lieutenant Henry and Jake Barnes, Harry Morgan's stance is not one of passive isolation, but one of active rebellion. For Morgan, life is still treacherous; it still "kills the very good and the very gentle and the very brave impartially." In fact, Morgan is beset on every side by forces that make it impossible for him to earn an honest living for himself and threaten the dignity and masculinity from which he draws strength and pride. But Harry is conscious of a code of behavior by which he may combat the world's injustice instead of acquiescing to it. The manhood of the bullfighter—his courage and skill and indomitability—provides a means of meeting head-on the immeasurable cruelty of things and of asserting himself in spite of the world. In short, Harry is the first major Hemingway protagonist to act out dramatically the author's vision of the majestic life and death of the matador, "who even though they were going directly to the grave (which is what makes any story a tragedy if carried out until the end) managed to put up a very fine performance en route" (DA, 233).

Hemingway establishes early in the novel the fact that Harry Morgan has been victimized by the prevailing patterns of an industrialized society. The only thing that prevents him from digging in the sewers with his friends on relief is his determination to make a more dignified living for himself as a charter fisherman. When that fails him and he is confronted with the alternatives of taking work he finds degrading or engaging in dangerous smuggling activities, he turns outlaw rather than compromise his simple sense of his own dignity and masculinity. He sums up his dilemma thus:

> I could sell the house and we could rent until I got some kind of work. What kind of work? No kind of work. I could go down to the bank and squeal now and what would I get? Thanks. Sure. Thanks. One bunch of Cuban government bastards cost me my arm shooting at me with a load when they had no need to and another bunch of U.S. ones took my boat. Now I can give up my home and get thanks. No thanks. The hell with it, he thought. I got no choice in it. (*HHN*, 148)

At another point Harry reasons:

> I don't want to fool with it but what choice have I got? They don't give you any choice now. I can let it go; but what will the next thing be? I didn't ask for any of this and if you've got to do it you've got to do it. (*HHN*, 105)

Working on Harry's pride, a companion reminds him:

> You're making seven dollars and a half a week. You got three kids in school that are hungry at noon. You got a family that their bellies hurt and I give you a chance to make a little money. (*HHN*, 95)

Finally, Harry decides "I'd just as soon go if there's any money in it." "I've got no boat, no cash, I got no education," he thinks. "What can a one-armed man work at? All I've got is my *cojones* to peddle" (*HHN*, 147).[2]

It is precisely because Harry does have *cojones* to peddle that he has "no choice in it." Like those defiant Spaniards examined in earlier chapters, Harry has *cojones*—Hemingway's Spanish symbol for manliness and integrity—and must prevail on his own terms

no matter what the cost. Philip Young notes that the book is "packed
with praise for his *cojones*," and W. M. Frohock remarks "how
plainly *cojones* symbolize the kind of integrity Hemingway admires"
in *To Have And Have Not*.[3] The concept of *cojones* is the foundation
upon which the ideal constitution of Hemingway's future heroes
is built. It is an all-embracing force—equivalent in nature to the
senequismo spoken of by Ganivet in *Idearium Espanol*—dominating
the personality of Hemingway's heroes and coloring his entire moral
view. Ganivet summed up this force in these words:

> Do not allow anything alien to your spirit to conquer you; in the
> midst of life's struggles, believe that you have within you a source
> of strength, something powerful and indestructible, something like
> a jeweled shaft . . . and regardless of the events that may involve
> you . . . remain so firm and erect that the least we can say of you
> is that you are a man.

Ganivet points out that the problem with such a moral view
is that it is severely limited. It becomes the yardstick used by the
Spanish (hence, by Hemingway, consciously or unconsciously) to
measure not only his own actions, but also those of all other human
beings. He concludes that this inflexible framework upon which
the Spanish moral character rests is largely to blame for the Spaniard's inability to associate or relate ideas. Hence, says Ganivet,
he is unable to integrate his ideas with sufficient clarity to produce
a definite, clear-cut conclusion or course of action. Just this condition—this simple-minded, physical response to complexity—
seemingly makes it impossible for Harry Morgan and Hemingway's
other later heroes to obtain a coherent view of their problems and
to gain a true perspective on their natures. An interesting speculation is whether the author, himself, was of so primitive a cast
of mind that he too saw no other response to the complex issues
confronting his characters than that dictated by *particularismo* and
senequismo.

Throughout the book, Harry Morgan attempts to realize values
of *pundonor* and *particularismo*. First of all, he plays out his hand
alone, living out the individualistic code of the matador. His pride
and fierce independence force him to disavow help from those

around him. Refusing to take his first mate with him on a dangerous smuggling mission, he affirms, "I wouldn't carry him the way things were now" (*HHN*, 38). "I got to have somebody I can depend on," he reminds himself (*HHN*, 105), but he concludes, "It would be better alone, anything is better alone but I don't think I can handle it alone. It would be much better alone" (*HHN*, 105). Ultimately, Harry decides that he must rely solely on his own resources because "I wouldn't trust anybody" (*HHN*, 133). "I have to do it alone, he thought" (*HHN*, 198).

Harry's insistence on doing things alone, in his own way, according to the dictates of his own conscience, is the same spirit of anarchistic independence that Unamuno said caused the Spanish people to be continually engaging in self-devouring activities—"waging a cruel war against one another . . . dismembering and destroying their enemies" (see page 45). It is, he remarks, the same spirit that is demonstrated in his countrymen's morbid and bloodthirsty interest in the barbaric slaughter of the bullring. The Spaniard's *particularismo* and *senequismo* he saw as inseparable from this tendency to violence and cruelty. It is this spirit that breeds a personal attitude of belligerence in Hemingway's last four heroes and activates their potential for incivility and bestiality.

Another aspect of Harry's *pundonor* is exhibited spectacularly throughout the novel and is closely allied to his spirit of *particularismo*. Harry and the reader are at all times aware of Harry's masculine capabilities that set him apart from the people in the world around him who have "wrecked," the leisure-class wastrels who manage to bear life only by drugging themselves on sex and liquor. In stark contrast to the feeling of helplessness and defeatism that characterized Frederick Henry and Jake Barnes, Harry Morgan asserts his inviolable manhood in conspicuous ways throughout the novel. Referring to Harry's extreme self-possession, one character remarks, after Harry has described a shooting incident to him, "You seem awfully sure about it" (*HHN*, 8).[4] Later on, Harry again demonstrates a certitude uncharacteristic of earlier Hemingway protagonists. Forced to decide about the fate of his first mate, he says, "I was sorry for him and for what I knew I'd have to do"

(*HHN*, 43).⁵ Further along, Harry contemplates his facility for control and right action in a way that summons up the image of the bullfighter measuring his opponent and planning his strategy in the bullring. "And I'm figuring all the time," he says, after a rigorous analysis of his situation. "I've got to think right all the time. I can't make a mistake. Not a mistake. Not once" (*HHN*, 106, 107). "I got confidence," he finally concludes. "That's the only thing I have got" (*HHN*, 126).

In addition to Morgan's insistence upon his isolated individualism and his instinctive sureness, he demonstrates a capacity for stoic endurance akin to Belmonte's in the Pamplona bullring. Probably no Hemingway protagonist to date has been so preoccupied with bravery and correct bearing, or so made to exhibit almost melodramatic shows of bravado. Talking about Harry's complete disregard for danger, a harbor authority remarks: "So Harry crossed last night. That boy's got *cojones*. He must have got that whole blow. . . . Damned if I'd cross a night like last night. Damned if I'd ever run liquor from Cuba" (*HHN*, 78).

This reckless indifference to the consequences of intense and dangerous action has become for Hemingway the "new system of belief" that Robert Jordan refers to in *For Whom The Bell Tolls*. Disregarding the normal safeguards to health becomes a way of achieving fulfillment within the framework of inevitable tragedy. The problem with such a philosophy is that it presages moral and physical disaster by forcing its followers into living a kind of perpetual *corrida*, a grim game in which life can only be made worthwhile by facing violence and death. Since man is impotent to challenge the injustice that rules the world, Hemingway reasons that one might as well squander his life out of a sense of defiance. The implications of such a philosophy are born out in the persons of Colonel Cantwell and the old Spaniard in "A Clean Well-Lighted Place." ⁶

The very beginning of the novel shows that Harry is too thick-skinned to be scared very easily. "Listen," he tells someone who threatens him, "Don't be so tough so early in the morning. I'm sure you've cut plenty people's throats. I haven't had my coffee yet." When Harry is wounded running illegal liquor, the stoical way in which he bears his pain is contrasted dramatically with the wailing of his companion. Disregarding his own pain, Harry tells him, "Take it easy," and while the companion "blubbered with his face against a sack," Harry "went on slowly lifting the sacked packages of liquor and dropping them over the side" (*HHN*, 75). He reflects "that he had never really felt pain before," and, "If I keep it out straight, pulled out straight, it don't hurt so bad" (*HHN*, 74). Then he goes through his pain uncomplaining.

> He felt very shaky now and he sat down on the steering seat and held his right arm tight between his thighs. His knees were shaking and with the shaking he could feel the ends of the bone in his upper arm grate. He opened his knees, lifted his arm out, and let it hang by his side. (*HHN*, 77)

Later, Hemingway says, "he lay quietly and took it" (*HHN*, 175). Near the end of the novel, an old embattled soldier speaks about the nobility of people like himself and Harry who have had to learn the value of simple fortitude.

> "Because we are the desperate ones," the man said. "The ones with nothing to lose. We are the completely brutalized ones. We're worse than the stuff the original Spartacus worked with. But it's tough to try to do anything with because we have been beaten so far that the only solace is booze and the only pride is in being able to take it." (*HHN*, 206)

But then the old veteran adds, "There are some of us that are going to hand it out" (*HHN*, 206).

Harry Morgan, indeed, has learned to "hand it out" as well as to take it. His renunciation of authority and absolute dependence upon his own manhood for support have, in fact, turned him into a belligerent and pugnacious individual. He is, to be sure, a brutalized man who, despite his better inclinations, evinces a sense of pleasure in doling out punishment. Once, Harry smacks a friend in the mouth after a mild argument, and when the shocked friend asks, "What did you have to hit me for?" Harry answers, "So you'd believe it" (*HHN*, 38). Later on, Harry describes his cruel

treatment of the harmless little Mr. Sing (the reason for which
is never really made clear) with undisguised zeal.

> I got his arm around behind him and came up on it but I brought
> it too far because I felt it go. When it went he made a funny little
> noise and came forward, me holding him throat and all, and bit
> me in the shoulder. But when I felt the arm go I dropped it. It
> wasn't any good to him any more and I took him by the throat
> with both hands, and brother, that Mr. Sing would flop just like
> a fish, true, his loose arm flailing. But I got him forward onto his
> knees and had both thumbs well in behind his talk-box, and I
> bent the whole thing back until she cracked. Don't think you can't
> hear it crack, either. (*HHN*, 53, 54)

Several times people close to Harry remark that he hardly seems
human. "You don't care what happens to a man," his mate says
to him (*HHN*, 69).[7] When the wounded mate comments "I couldn't
feel no worse," Harry adds cheerfully, "You'll feel worse when
the old doctor probes for it," and the mate says, "You ain't human,"
"You ain't got human feelings" (*HHN*, 86). Later, a long-time friend
explains about Harry that "since he was a boy he never had no
pity for nobody. But he never had no pity for himself either" (*HHN*,
98).

Near the end of the novel, Harry engages in what is to become
a commonplace occupation for the last four Hemingway protagonists—a dialogue with himself and with others on the necessity
of killing, which is a final manifestation of the aggressive instinct
that prevails in these later Hemingway heroes. After a grim prelude
of a dozen pages of steady conversation about the values of killing,
Harry is finally worked up to a point of bestiality at which he
feels himself capable of the bloody job of gunning down his four
passengers. "Now's as good as any time, he said to himself. No
sense waiting now" (*HHN*, 169). Thinking about the deed, "his
whole insides were cold," but by the time he has machine-gunned
his adversaries to death, "all the cold was gone from around his
heart now and he had the old hollow singing feeling" (*HHN*, 171).
His next act is to put the muzzle of the gun against the head of
one man he particularly did not like and to blast away at it.

Motivated by the bullfighter's ethics, Harry Morgan, primitive, fiercely proud and independent, is denied the path of docility and compromise; only through violence that brings about his death can he affirm his dignity and manhood. And for Harry Morgan, death is preferable to surrendering to the powers in modern society that deprive one of dignity and honor. Pervading the novel is the sense that Harry would like to cooperate with those around him, and herein lies his essential tragedy—the frustration of his great need for solidarity and interdependence. Because he can find no consolation in the ravaged lives of those around him, he turns to the excessive individualism of the matador for strength and courage. Belligerent and tragically self-absorbed, his life becomes a perfect example of the hermetically sealed compartment that Ortega y Gasset talks about. Instead of cultivating human intercourse in order to make his life more meaningful, he remains scornful of authority and organization, and aloof and superior to the people around him. Thus cut off from chances for communication with his fellow human beings, he becomes increasingly resentful and recklessly defiant and gives way to the tendency to violence and cruelty that eventually ends his life.

At the end of the novel, Harry Morgan realizes that his bellicosity and individualistic motivation have failed him, but the pattern of his tragic isolation and death has been set and his recognition of the need for human solidarity comes too late. With the words Harry speaks, "No matter how a man alone ain't got no bloody chance," Hemingway introduces a conflict that is to become increasingly acute in the minds of his next three protagonists. Apparently, Hemingway had begun at this time to become aware of the tragic effects of the pattern of rebellion, individualism, and isolation that he had formerly extolled in the lives of his matadors. In any case, several critics have interpreted in the final words of Harry Morgan a renunciation on the author's part of rebellious, anti-social, and belligerently individual attitudes and the acceptance of a new social framework. Edgar Johnson, in his "Farewell The Separate Peace," feels that Hemingway means to show that Harry Morgan "has been beaten because he has tried to stand alone and fight alone," and

that this provides the "clue to victory" for his heroes to come.[8]
"Hemingway has rejected a philosophy of atomic individualism,"
he says. "He has fought his way out of defeatism. . . . For the
good, the gentle and the brave, he now tells us, if they do not
try to stand alone and make a separate peace, defeat is not inevitable."[9] And Maxwell Geismar says, "It is within this pattern of
Hemingway's renunciation, exile, and return that his latest and
most popular novel, For Whom The Bell Tolls, must be appraised." [10]

As these critics suggest, Hemingway's last three heroes do indeed
evince a desire to realize the interdependence and human solidarity
first experienced by Harry Morgan at the end of To Have And
Have Not. Yet the attempts of these men to modify their aggressive
tendencies and to dissociate themselves from the scornful and
rebellious life-style of the matador prove totally unsuccessful. What
results is extreme mental suffering and feelings of guilt, and the
agonized coexistence of warring forces that creates the powerful
source of tension within their characters.

In For Whom The Bell Tolls there are no longer any literal bullfighters; yet Hemingway is as much preoccupied with the bullfighter's values as ever, and the conflict in his hero's mind between
the forces of aggression and restraint, individualism and interdependence, increases in severity. The author states that in this
novel he is putting all that he had learned in the years before
about the Spaniard's character and his values: "It was everything
I had learned about Spain for eighteen years." [11] And Robert Jordan
emphasizes that the Spanish civil war was his education. "It is
part of one's education," he says. "It will be quite an education
when it's finished. You learn in this war if you listen. You most
certainly did" (FWBT, 76). What Hemingway and Jordan appear
to have learned at this point from their respective educations is
that the Spaniard's anarchistic rebellion against authority and his
rampant, often arrogant individualism are an unsuccessful means
of combatting the world's injustice.

In one sense, For Whom The Bell Tolls reads like a morality play,
with the forces of restraint and aggression battling for Robert
Jordan's soul. All of the members of Pablo's band display the

extremist tendencies inherent in the Spaniard's nature as described by Unamuno,[12] with the bloodthirsty Pablo at one pole and the tender minded Anselmo at the other. Consequently, Jordan is torn by the two warring impulses that cause a constant drain on his energies—the impulse to love human beings and allow himself to become involved with them, as in his good companionship with Anselmo or his love for Maria, and the impulse to engage in the rebellious individualism of the matador, such as is evinced by the fanatical hater Augustín and the irresponsible anarchist Pablo. Jordan exhibits a spiritual relationship with both of these extremes; by turns, he is both gentle and cruel, tender and barren of feeling. He looks with regret upon the frequent reversions to bestiality in the people around him and reflects painfully on the pathological aspect of much that is irrationally aggressive within himself. And in particular he observes that the Spaniard's wilful resistance to authority and domination is the chief disintegrating factor in his struggle for a better life. Yet ultimately, he acquiesces to the necessity for cruelty and destruction.

Seemingly, for a long time Robert Jordan has been intellectually naive about the people he is fighting with—the supposedly devoted and idealistic adherents of the Republican cause. He is so actively devoted, himself, to the establishment of a more harmonious human community that he blinds himself to the internal failings of the Spanish character that exclude any chance of achieving universal brotherhood. Lionel Trilling points out that Jordan has no awareness of the badness of his friends, and that he believes solidly in his guerrillas with their strange, virtuous Indian-talk.[13]

Robert Jordan knows that he may die fighting for the Republican cause in Spain, but his sense of involvement allows him to come to terms with his death in these words: "I have fought for what I believed in for a year now. If we win here we will win everywhere. The world is a fine place and worth the fighting for and I hate very much to leave it" (FWBT, 446). Later, Jordan is shown to be as much aware as Manuel García Maera or any of Hemingway's matadors of the value of dying well, with courage and style, but he is also aware of the additional value of dying for a moral cause, risking his life for an ideal worth dying for. To this end Jordan reflects:

> This ideal gave you a part in something that you could believe in wholly and completely and in which you felt an absolute brotherhood with the others who were engaged in it. It was something that you have never known before but that you had experienced now and you gave such importance to it and the reason for it that your own death seemed of complete unimportance. (*FWBT*, 235)

Despite Jordan's hopes for a wider realization of brotherhood, however, his underlying sense of the self-destructive impulses of the Spanish—of the hatred, violence, and cruelty and steadily mounting sadism that was undermining the Republican cause—dramatically contradicts his newly avowed faith in humanity. But only when he is monstrously overwhelmed with the cynicism and shameful acts of betrayal and cruelty among his comrades can he allow himself to glimpse the true nature of those militant forces in the Spanish character that are leading inevitably to defeat. Jordan's love for the Spanish people, about whom he plans to write an optimistic book, is simply so great that he cannot bring himself easily to judge or deal with their shortcomings.[14]

Maxwell Geismar writes about the tragic paradox confronting Robert Jordan, "as the story progresses . . . the 'Yes' of Jordan is progressively minimized by the submerged *nada* of his creator." And, in addition, by the pervasive *nada* of his comrades, as well. Jordan's emotional attachment to the Spanish people is first shaken when he hears Pilar's account of the murder of the Fascists in the village square at the hands of Pablo's mob. The pillaging of the Fascist town is perhaps more coldly brutal than any previous episode in Hemingway's work, and the killing of the Fascists by the anarchist Pablo is needlessly cruel.[15] Even though Pilar seems to detect the furious mixture of humanity and bestiality among the killers, she recounts the spectacle with a cold fascination, as if it had been a bullfight; and, in fact, the barbaric spectacle perpetrated by Jordan's friends brings forth the same primitive passions—the same zest for killing—as are inspired by the primitive ceremony of killing epitomized in the bullring.[16]

Jordan appears to recognize the tragic implications of the brutal and senseless slaughter of the Fascists—that it was a time more for the explosion of irrational and primitive emotions than a time to seek justice. Given the opportunity to vent their true feelings, once they taste blood through the murder of the first Fascist, Pablo's band turns the executions into a mass murder, characterized by revolting butchery and pure savagery. Howling in a great collective voice and worked up by the smell of blood and burst bowels and bloody entrails, they grow more impatient for the next victim, the next bull. One drunkard summarizes the sentiments of the crowd when he yells, "Qué salga el toro! Let the bull out."

The inordinate lust revealed in the brutality of the sadistic execution no doubt causes Jordan to wonder about the brutalized condition of his friends, but he does not allow himself to reflect on this in any serious way. He seems fairly content to accept Pilar's conclusion that the killing of the Fascists was ultimately necessary. He does not balk when she rationalizes that the executions were necessary because apathy had let the social situation in the villages of Spain deteriorate so far that such mob action was the only recourse for the underdogs. Her final consolation is that, after all, they were only doing what had been done to them by the Fascists, which is similar to the rationalization on the part of the author in *Green Hills Of Africa* that it was all right to make others suffer since he himself had suffered greatly.

In similar fashion, Robert Jordan and Anselmo, the sweet man of peace in the midst of war's horrors, rationalize away similar stirrings of conscience throughout the novel. Repeatedly, Anselmo searches his conscience about the right to kill. He believes killing to be a sin, but he decides that killing is necessary to win the war. And so, even though he "wishes to win the war and shoot nobody," he does his duty as a staunch supporter of the Republic. In like manner, Jordan concludes that it is "all right to take another man's life if it is to prevent something worse happening to other people" (*FWBT*, 198). At one point he asks himself during a fit of guilt: "Don't you know it is wrong to kill?" "Yes," he answers himself. "But you do it. Yes" (*FWBT*, 264).

Despite the acts of grossness and cruelty, Jordan seeks to justify the sins of his spiritual brothers by invoking the necessity for cruelty and violence in the fight for universal justice:

> Neither you nor this old man is anything. You are instruments to do your duty. There are necessary orders that are no fault of yours and there is a bridge and that bridge can be the point on which the future of the human race may turn. (*FWBT*, 43)

Jordan has other ways by which he assuages his spiritual discomfort over killing. Early in the novel, experiencing his first pangs of guilt, he thinks, "Turn off the thinking now, old timer, old comrade. You're a bridge-blower now. Not a thinker" (*FWBT*, 15). Later, he rationalizes endangering the *guerrillero* band: "You have no responsibility for them except in action. The orders do not come from you. They come from Golz. . . . But should a man carry out impossible orders knowing what they lead to?" (*FWBT*, 142).[17] Jordan resolves his conflict through the belief that the responsibility for an act is placed upon the one who orders the act done rather than upon the one performing it. He believes that his innocence can be maintained by following orders, by "doing anything that I am ordered."

Jordan, though believing that following orders is sufficient justification for killing, still *defers* rather than *displaces* his guilt and final responsibility. He realizes that he will have to make judgments "afterwards" in order to function effectively. Since the premium is on utility rather than integrity in war, Robert Jordan manages to fulfill his function through detachment. He will, he tells himself, write a book about the war. He is the college teacher who is fighting a war for a while, but who is still a college teacher. Though he kills, he does not regard himself as more of a killer than a college teacher. He is fighting in the war of his own volition. And this allows him to achieve sufficient distance from its horrors to function guiltlessly—at least for its duration. But even though Jordan manages to fight a war by avoiding a direct confrontation in which he might have to face and accept the impact of his actions, he sees that killing "is a great sin and that afterwards we must do something very strong to atone for it" (FWBT, 196).

In the struggle between the forces of aggression and restraint for Jordan's soul, the battle is one-sided: the force of violence and bloodlust was bound, it seems, to exert the greater pull on his character. The instinct in those around him for inflicting violence upon others is too prevalent to resist. To this end, Malcolm Cowley has observed, "Hemingway himself seems to have a feeling for half-forgotten sacraments," such as the Spaniard's instinct for killing. "His cast of mind is pre-Christian and prelogical," says Cowley.[18] Thus Jordan sympathizes with Augustín when he speaks of the necessity to kill that was on him like "on a mare in heat," and remarks that there is no stronger thing in life. Thinking this over, Jordan calls it the Spanish "extra sacrament" that, repressed by Christianity, has welled forth in wars and inquisitions; and he admits that he too and "all who are soldiers by choice have enjoyed it at some time whether they lie about it or not" (FWBT, 428). This primitive emotion is precisely what Jake Barnes enjoyed in connection with death-giving in The Sun Also Rises and Hemingway explained more clearly in Death In The Afternoon—the pagan elation of one "still in rebellion against death." And it is again this pervasive religious ecstasy of killing that seems to give consolation to Robert Jordan as he performs his soldier's duty at the end of the novel, reverting to the primitive ceremony of killing as epitomized in the bullring.

Before examining the ecstasy that the act of killing seems to excite in Jordan's primitive soul, first note that it is not the pull of militant ethics and barbaric emotions alone that thwarts Jordan's efforts to achieve communion and "the feeling of absolute brotherhood" he so desperately seeks. For, along with the bloodlust and sadism, Jordan's comrades in arms demonstrate no true desire for brotherhood. The lessons Jordan learns about the prideful and anarchistic temperament of his Spanish brothers while fighting for the good life teaches him only the futility of achieving any kind of lasting and meaningful connection with his fellow man. *For Whom The Bell Tolls* is filled not with scenes of communion and brotherhood, but with those of emotional and psychological isolation and disunity. Whether it is El Sordo's band surrounded and isolated and doomed on the hilltop, Jordan waiting hopelessly alone by his machine gun, or Anselmo alone and guilt-ridden at the bridge, the novel depicts one forlorn individual after another, surrounded by omens of death and disintegration.

Far from realizing the ideal embodied in John Donne's contention that "No man is an Island," Jordan's friends are all islands within themselves, destined to live and die alone in corrosive solitude. The impression is given that the Spaniards' inability to join together for a common cause stretches all the way from the higher echelons in Madrid down to the gypsy Raphael, who is so irresponsible that he runs off to shoot rabbits when he should be standing guard near Pablo's cave. This particular failing is summed up at the end of the novel when the Russian General Golz refers to the futility of the Spanish offensive: "You know how those people are" (*FWBT*, 428).

Jordan, himself, knows about this aspect of the Spanish character. Learning about the Spaniard's narrow provincialism—about his destructive spirit of *particularismo*—has been part of the "education" he spoke of. He knows that he would never have been accepted among them had he not been one of them at heart. "They trusted you on understanding the language completely and speaking it idiomatically and having a knowledge of the different places," he says. "A Spaniard was only really loyal to his village in the end. First Spain of course, then his own tribe, then his province, then his village, his family and finally his trade. . . ." Then Jordan reflects, "He never felt like a foreigner," and adds, "only when they turned on you." But he concludes: "This was no way to think" (*FWBT*, 135). Finally, Jordan identifies the betrayal and tragic disunity in the Loyalist forces that have destroyed his faith in humanity once again:

> Of course they turned on you. They turned on you often but they always turned on everyone. They turned on themselves, too. If

you had three together, two would unite against one, and then the two would start to betray each other. Not always, but often enough for you to take enough cases and start to draw it as a conclusion. (*FWBT*, 135) [19]

It seems that by this time even the idealistic Jordan's faith in his people has begun to drop away. He is much like the young apprenticed torero, Joaquín, who, when the spectre of death and mutilation on El Sordo's hilltop becomes too grim to bear, can no longer get the words out that signify his faith in the cause. As if the hero had come full circle from the predicament of Frederick Henry in *A Farewell To Arms*, he once more is threatened by the force which kills the very good and the very brave and the very gentle impartially. His sense of inevitable defeat arouses once more his exaggerated consciousness of the treachery and cruelty in the world around him.

Ultimately, the failure of the establishment of the human community that Jordan has sought causes him to resume the old familiar pose of the rebellious individualist, and at the end of the novel Jordan dismally retreats behind the protective aggression and ego-centric stance of the matador. Jordan knows that his chances for a meaningful relationship with his fellow human beings is gone, but, by giving himself completely to the rigid set of rules for war and for the attainment of manhood, he can still impart some sense of form and dignity to his life. And so Jordan, in the last chapter of the novel, engages in a tortured debate with himself about the ethics of dying and killing. "There are many worse things than this," he says, contemplating his death (*FWBT*, 466). "You are not afraid of it once you know you have to do it, are you? No, he said truly."

> Who do you suppose has it easier? Ones with religion or just taking it straight? It comforts them very much but we know there is no thing to fear. It is only missing it that's bad. Dying is only bad when it takes a long time and hurts so much that it humiliates you. (*FWBT*, 468)

All the signs of the matador are there as Jordan awaits his inevitable doom. Jordan plays out his lone hand like all those matadors Hemingway admired in the past. Despite his lofty claims about dying for the sake of human solidarity, the chief driving force in Jordan's final response to death is fierce personal pride and vanity. Looking through the eyes of the torero, he dies not on behalf of the grand cause of human liberation, but in keeping with the Spanish belief that there is very definitely a correct way to live and a correct way to die, and that the grand manner of the dying may demonstrate man's indomitability beyond his physical destruction. Going through his pain, with no one to call on for help, Jordan remarks, "he felt that much more alone" (*FWBT*, 466). And when the pain becomes unbearable, his manly pride and his sense of the nobility of dying well provides him the fortitude to endure. "I will take whatever I get," he says (*FWBT*, 469). For a moment he considers compromising with his integrity and killing himself before he has conquered his adversary—the approaching Fascist soldiers. "The leg, where the big nerve had been bruised by the fall, was hurting badly now," he thinks, so "why wouldn't it be all right to just do it now and then the whole thing would be over with?" "I think it would be all right to do it now? Don't you?" (*FWBT*, 470). But he answers, "No, it isn't." "I'm against that," he says. Then, defying the pain, he grins and jokes, "I ought to carry a spare leg" (*FWBT*, 469). Reconciled to bearing the pain, Jordan reflects with self-conscious pride, "I'd like to tell grandfather about this one. I'll bet he never had to go over and find a show like this." "How do you know?" his other self questions. "He may have done fifty." "No," Jordan proudly assures himself, "Be accurate. Nobody did any fifty like this one. Nobody did five. Nobody did one maybe not just like this" (*FWBT*, 469).

Jordan dies, then, much in the style of the matador, separated from the "maine" by his *particularismo*, going through his pain with a show of grand endurance and asserting his indomitability till the very end. Like the Romeros and Maeras, men alone against the world, he tries to face his final moment of truth with dignity and courage, happy with his fierce pride on display. He is left, at the close of the novel, working alone, keeping himself under control before his bull, showing himself superior to circumstances until the final thrusting of the sword. "Robert Jordan lay behind the tree," Hemingway writes, "holding onto himself very carefully and delicately to keep his hands steady" (*FWBT,* 471). And in a final gesture of defiance and affirmation, watching the enemy come into his rifle sights, Jordan's heart pounds wildly and he asserts, "I've held it. I held it all right" (*FWBT,* 470).

7 / Performance en Route to Death: Part Two The Spanish Element in Colonel Cantwell and Santiago

IN THIS agonized coexistence of warring forces in the minds of Hemingway's last four heroes, Colonel Cantwell, the aging hero of *Across The River And Into The Trees* (1950), is the least able to achieve an equilibrium between the will to kindness and gentleness and the impulse to aggression and egocentrism. Of the four men, he appears most tortured by the schizophrenic split in his nature. He experiences profound pangs of guilt as a result of his long association with killing; yet the more militant side of his nature asserts itself until finally he is led to his own self-destruction. Cantwell has no illusions about subduing what he calls his "wild-boar blood"—his will to aggression, which distinguishes him so much from Hemingway's pre-Spanish heroes. What is left for Cantwell is to learn how to live with his tragic aloneness—to play out his lone hand with the militant fortitude of the embittered and aging matador.

Colonel Cantwell is clearly an extension of Hemingway's Spanish-oriented heroes. The author, himself, established this fact by remarking to Gary Cooper that he should play the role of Cantwell because "you'd just be playing Robert Jordan ten years older." [1] He bears an even closer resemblance, however, to Manuel Garcia, the old bullfighter in "The Undefeated," and to Manuel García Maera, the bullfighter whom Hemingway said in *Death In The Afternoon* was the greatest of them all. Cantwell's particular dilemma, like that of Manuel Garcia, is that he has splurged his life away through contact with violence and death, but is old now and no longer able to continue at the same dangerous pace. Despite the fact that Manuel Garcia's coordination of hand and eye had decreased, his pride demanded that he pursue his trade without asking any favors or making any concessions to his age. In like fashion, the chief cause of the Colonel's bitterness and the thing he rebels hardest against is his loss of vitality. Like the stout-hearted Manuel, Cantwell is bitter because, despite the disintegration of his body, his spirit is still more willing than ever.

Cantwell finds that death by old age is a particular horror he had not counted on. Like the matador, he has long been used to facing death violently from the outside. But life for the Colonel simply comes to an end because his spent organism refuses him further service. When the book opens, he has just suffered a heart attack and he knows death is imminent. Hence, the one thing that has given his life meaning, his work—the trade of making war, which was for him an art form—has been denied him. "I'm not lonely when I'm working," he says, "I have to think too hard to ever be lonely." "But you are not working now," admonishes an inner voice (ART, 104). And throughout the book he is increasingly aware of his waning powers. "I'm getting awfully slow, he thought. Somebody will take me any day now" (ART, 41). For Cantwell, "getting slow" spells the end of his capabilities as a skillful soldier, and, like the matador who has outlived his talent, who can no longer be good, he realizes his uselessness and what it is he must do.

The full horror of Cantwell's dilemma is perhaps best illustrated through Hemingway's "A Clean Well-Lighted Place." Like the old man in that story, Cantwell, in the final days of his life, makes no move whatever to become aware of the hopeless void within him or to seek a cure. Because both men can no longer assert their *pundonor* in some spectacular fashion, life is meaningless for them. A safe assumption is that the old man in "A Clean Well-Lighted Place" was as rebellious as Cantwell in his youth, but now he cannot act out his rebellion against the forces of *nada* through excess of drinking, love making, war making, and so forth. Now he has nothing to look forward to but thoughts of death and nothingness. Having splurged his life away with no thought of the future, the burned out old man invokes the mechanical aspects of the bullfighter's code to help him combat his fear of the horror of nothingness. But the prospect of inevitable suffering is too much for him and he contemplates suicide as an answer.

Cantwell's lifelong indifference to the consequences of intense and dangerous action, his commitment to the "now," has bred self-absorption and allowed him no time for an examination of his own conscience. Unamuno refers to this typically Spanish pattern of living as the "gangrena del alma española"—because, since there is no challenge to the individual demanding extended mental activity, it lessens the possibility of establishing relationships that will keep the mental life alive when the senses no longer serve. Here lies the crux of Cantwell's dilemma. Having always lived by seizing the intensity of the moment, the activities of peace and the relationships and pursuits of normal life are no longer possible for the old Colonel. The only moments of value are those with a background of pending disaster, of extreme stress. And these can be had now only at the expense of almost certain death.

Hemingway could not have paid a greater tribute to the proud and defiant figure of Manuel Maera than by fashioning the character of Colonel Cantwell. With his heart condition, his reckless commitment to action, his lightheadedness and loose morals, and his total lack of desire for health, he is the reincarnation of the man who displays all the essential virtues Hemingway admired. Cantwell, like Maera, will not slow down, but wilfully burns himself out "not as an act of bravado, but from choice" (DA, 79). Cantwell attempts to live out his remaining days with just the rebellious attitudes of Maera, continuing to hunt, to drink, to love, and to live disdainful of consequences—even though he knows he is hastening his death. In short, he goes to the bull when the bull will no longer come to him, "arrogant, dominating and disregarding danger." He still clings to his bullfighter's values, which, despite their ill effect on him, are all he has left. Retaining the determination of the Manuels and Maeras to last and to play his hand out the best he can, he concludes: "I know where I'm going . . . better to die on our feet than to live on our knees . . . better to live one day as a lion than a hundred years as a sheep" (ART, 40).

Quite clearly, Cantwell has become callous and brutalized in spirit from his many years' association with death. He reminisces about the senseless and brutal killings he has witnessed as if the people involved were nothing more than obstacles. And some sights, some memories the Colonel cannot stop thinking about however hard he tries. For instance, there is the horrible report of a dead GI lying in the middle of the road who has been run over repeatedly by passing vehicles, and the Colonel remembers "just how he felt, lifting him, and how he had been flattened and the strangeness of the flatness" (ART, 257). And, again, he recalls:

> There was one other thing, I remember. We had put an awful lot of white phosphorous on the town before we got in for good. . . . That was the first time I ever saw a German dog eating a roasted German kraut. Later on I saw a cat working on him too. (ART, 257)

Death has been close to the Colonel all his life and he speaks of it with the disrespect central to the rebellious attitude of the matador. "Death is a lot of shit, he thought," and he contemplates the grim fact that "I have lived with it nearly all my life and the dispensing of it has been my trade" (ART, 220). The Colonel acknowledges what living with it nearly all his life has done to him when he looks at himself in the mirror and observes, "the cruelty and resolution showed in his large eyes as clearly as when the hooded muzzle of a tank swung toward you" (ART, 223), or, as Hemingway may well have had in mind, the muzzle of a bull.

Ultimately, the Colonel finds that he has been too long habituated to the primitive and warlike stance of the matador—the professional warrior—to change his militant ways; yet, ironically, he exhibits a clearer insight into his own nature and a greater stirring of conscience than any previous Hemingway hero. "I've been a sorry son of a bitch many times," he remarks. "Why can I not suspend this trade of arms and be a kind and good man as I would have wished to be. . . . I should be a better man with less wildboar blood in the small time which remains" (*ART*, 210). Later he says, "You do not want to kill anyone anymore; ever." But then, as if in hopeless acquiescence to his primitive cast of mind—to his bullfighter's pugnacity—he reminds himself: "Who are you feeding that to. . . . You going to run as a Christian. . . . Who wants to make a bet on that?" (*ART*, 291).

Throughout the novel, Cantwell evinces a need for confession; yet, when it comes, it is the strained and unconvincing confession of a blocked and despairing temperament. The Spanish-like code of manners, the stiff control of the facade, has so long prevented a healthy outlet of emotion that, as Horst Oppel observes, "he is little more than a phonograph record, sputtering forth out of that poor supply of words which five decades of living have left him." ² Renata, the Colonel's last love and confessor of sorts, knows that what he needs at the end of his life is "castigation" and "purgation." And she tries to draw the Colonel out so that he can purge his bitterness. It works for a time, but as soon as the Colonel realizes "he was not lecturing; he was confessing" (*ART*, 186), he withdraws in a rather bogus display of manly reserve and resists further promptings. "I don't need to purge," he says (*ART*, 188). Attempts to rescue the brutalized soldier from the constant preoccupation with his ego are futile. His *particularismo* has driven so far into his soul, has become so deeply embedded in his character, that a reversal now is impossible. A purely erotic relationship with Renata is the most he can hope for.

As was pointed out earlier, Cantwell eventually lapses into the strained and mirthless stoicism of the matador. Despite his insights into the destructive potential of his militant and self-centered pattern of behavior, he still has too much "wildboar truculence" and stubborn defiance in his nature to change himself or his life. As with Robert Jordan, he has been led further away from a share in that community spirit he professes to believe in and yearn for until, finally, only the contemplation of his own defiant death serves as a source of relief. Rather than live the perpetual horror of nothingness of the old man in "A Clean Well-Lighted Place," Cantwell seizes on the ultimate value of the bullfighter—the feeling of rebellion against death that comes from its administering—and performs his last act of aggression by running on the horns of the bull.

The goal here has been primarily to analyze rather than evaluate the effects of the Spanish influence on Hemingway's work. Yet it is appropriate at this point to note more emphatically what was hinted at earlier in the discussion of Harry Morgan. As with Harry, Cantwell is far more rigidly Spanish in make-up than Robert Jordan or Santiago. In Morgan and Cantwell the spirit of *particularismo* and *senequismo* is so dominant that the suffering man beneath the Spanish mask is nearly lost from sight. Thus, ironically, instead of the healthy tension that develops within the minds of Jordan and Santiago and the engaging complexity of their moral conflicts, Hemingway turns away from such subtlety in the case of Morgan and Cantwell and concentrates instead on their simple conflict with external environment.

All aspects of the matador's pattern of behavior discussed so far find expression in the story of old Santiago, *The Old Man And The Sea*. More isolated than ever from human contacts, this final edition of the Hemingway hero represents the epitome of the matador's rebellious and tragic individualism. "His choice," thought Santiago, "had been to stay in the deep dark water far out beyond all snares and treacheries. My choice was to go there to find him beyond all people. Beyond all people in the world. Now we are joined together and have been since noon. And no one to help either one of us" (*OMS*, 55). Yet, by the end of the novel, Santiago has had far greater success than Cantwell, Jordan, or Morgan in achieving a healthy coordination between the polarities existing in his character. Perhaps this is because old age has taught him to temper the prideful and anarchistic individualism of his youth. His newly gained humility appears to aid him in promoting a coordinated, harmonious state of mind in which the forces of love and peace and understanding predominate.

Santiago's spirit of *particularismo* is established at the very start of the novel. Because the old man has great pride in his individual superiority as a fisherman, he refuses help in attempting to bring

in a big fish after a tough year. Having gone eighty-four days
without a fish, Santiago has become more dependent upon the
young boy Manolo and upon his other friends in his village than
he is willing to admit. Clinton S. Burhans notes:

> The boy keeps up his confidence and hope, brings him clothes
> and such necessities as water and soap, and sees that he has fresh
> bait for his fishing. Martin, the restaurant owner, sends the old
> man food, and Perico, the wineshop owner, gives him newspapers
> so that he can read about baseball.[3]

But all of this charity the old man accepts with a sense of strain
befitting his fierce pride. He even refuses the young boy's offer
to leave the boat his parents have made him go in and return
to his. Still, on the morning of Santiago's last trip, Manolo arranges
for a nourishing breakfast and secures the fish and sardines that
Santiago will use for bait. He helps launch the skiff and sees
Santiago off in the dark with a wish for luck on his eighty-fifth
day.

Santiago's great pride also forces him to assert himself, disregarding danger, even though it may mean initiating his own destruction. His *pundonor* demands that he demonstrate his skill constantly, proving over and over his value as a man. With the same
self-conscious awareness of his own manhood that Robert Jordan
displayed facing death on a Spanish hillside, Santiago reflects:

> Although it is unjust, he thought . . . I will show him what a man
> can do and what a man endures. . . . I told the boy I was a
> strange old man. . . . Now is when I must prove it. The thousand
> times that he had proven it meant nothing. Now he was proving
> it again. Each time was a new time and he never thought about
> the past when he was doing it. (*OMS*, 73)

Santiago's spirit of *particularismo* and *pundonor* is directly related
to his pessimistic Spanish world view that the universe is a place
of inescapable violence where the great law of life is strife and
destruction: "everything kills everything else in some way," he
reflects. "Fishing kills me exactly as it keeps me alive" (*OMS*,
117). The old man identifies himself completely with the great

fish and other animals about him who are involved in the primitive struggle to survive. As he sails far out on the sea, he thinks of the sea "as feminine and as something that gave or withheld great favors" (*OMS*, 33). For the bird who rests on his line and for the other creatures who share with him such a capricious and violent life, the old man feels a deadly primal relationship—the relationship of the hunter and the hunted. As Hemingway, himself, had concluded in *Green Hills Of Africa*, Santiago believes that because they suffer a mutual condition of existence, it is all right to kill. "I killed him in self-defense," the old man tells himself, "and I killed him well" (*OMS*, 117).

Santiago believes that because life is hard, that because it is filled with "traps and treacheries"—unpredictable like the sea or a bad bull—he must be just as tough in order to survive with dignity and honor. In other words, he has adopted the rebellious and militant stance of the matador to establish his indomitability. And it is just this stance—the stubborn determination to endure on his own terms and the consequent refusal to enlist human help—that both sustains and destroys him during his great trial on the sea.

When the sharks come to finish off Santiago's great fish, the old man fights them off with a grand display of courage and endurance. Santiago is Pedro Romero, Manuel Garcia, and Manuel García Maera all rolled into one heroic image of the proud and stubborn matador. Everything that the matador represents to Hemingway is present in the old fisherman: the old tenacity, the omnipresent capacity for endurance, the refusal to be dominated, and the mastery of technique. Santiago, with his strained back and his cut and cramped left hand, is like Maera going on despite his pain, disregarding his broken wrist, going in for the sixth time over the horns of the bull. And just as Maera's bullfight terminated with the final sword thrust between the shoulders of the bull, Santiago's fight with the fish terminates with the final mastery of pain and the thrust of the harpoon into his opponent's heart.

Despite Santiago's resemblance to the familiar figure of the matador, they differ in one very crucial aspect: the way in which they accept defeat. Santiago comes to recognize what Robert Jordan is barely able to bring himself to admit and what Colonel Cantwell is unable to cope with—that his pride has made inaccessible to him the path of human brotherhood and led him instead into a state of solitude. Whereas the fatalistic acceptance of *particularismo* ultimately dooms Jordan and Cantwell to bitter isolation and death, Santiago is able to transcend the limitations of his temperament at the end of his life and to a certain degree establish contact with his fellow human beings.

Robert Jordan and Colonel Cantwell had the ability to shrug off stirrings of conscience and to rationalize pangs of guilt that is native to the Spanish character. But Santiago's capacity for self-criticism forces him to examine his actions more realistically. Thus, when he tries to delude himself that he killed the fish "to keep me alive and feed many people," his conscience informs him: "You did not kill the fish only to keep alive and to sell for food. . . . You killed him for pride and because you are a fisherman. You loved him when he was alive and you loved him after. If you love him, it is not a sin to kill him. Or is it more?" (*OMS*, 116).

Ultimately, Santiago rightly concludes that his real motivation for searching for and catching the big fish was pride—to show that he was still El Campeon. He senses that in going out too far he has ruined the fish and himself. "I should have not gone out so far, fish," he says. "Neither for you nor for me. I'm sorry, fish" (*OMS*, 73). Santiago knows that it is his great pride as a fisherman, his need to prove his manly capabilities that has driven him out beyond all people and brought upon himself and the great fish the forces of violence and destruction. Later on, he ponders his dilemma once again. "And what beat you?" he asks himself. "Nothing," answers a stern inner voice. "I went out too far." Urged on by pride, by the persistent rebelliousness in his nature, Santiago is defeated by antagonisms within his own temperament. But he knows this and is courageous enough to try to do something about it. Therein lies his margin of moral victory over a long line of tragically thwarted and embittered heroes.

As a result of his experience Santiago does not despair in the manner of earlier heroes; instead, he learns how deeply related he is to the rest of created life. He begins to feel a sense of friendship with and love for the great fish and with the other creatures who share with him such a capricious and violent life. When he sees a flight of wild ducks go over, the old man knows "no man was ever alone on the sea" (*OMS*, 67). And after he has caught and killed the great marlin whom he has come to pity and then to respect and then to love, he feels no pride of accomplishment, no sense of victory. Rather, he seems to feel almost as though he has betrayed the great fish: "I am only better than him through trickery," he thinks, "and he meant me no harm" (*OMS*, 99). In particular, his new humility, which for the first time in Hemingway's Spanish-oriented heroes has come to overshadow his arrogance and pride, is demonstrated through his relationship with the boy Manolo. When Santiago is forced into an introspective reverie to keep himself company on the vast and lonely sea, he realizes and becomes reconciled to the help and love and care of others that now keeps him alive: "The boy keeps me alive, he thought. I must not deceive myself too much" (*OMS*, 106). As his loneliness increases and his sense of isolation on the great sea intensifies, he reflects more and more on his dependence on the boy and on his other friends: "I cannot be too far out now, he thought. I hope no one has been too worried. . . . Many of the older fishermen will worry. Many others too, he thought. I live in a good town" (*OMS*, 115). As Santiago's ordeal becomes more trying, he longs for the company of the boy. "I wish I had the boy," he says, and his resolution tightens. Later the same night, he says aloud, "I wish the boy was here," and he is able to summon up additional strength for the fight still to come. The next day, when the old man thinks he can endure no longer, he thinks, "If the boy was here he would wet the coils of the line. . . . Yes. If the boy were here. If the boy were here" (*OMS*, 115).

Significantly enough, when Santiago returns from his ordeal he awakens in his shack and talks with his young assistant and notices "how pleasant it was to have someone to talk to instead of speaking only to himself and to the sea" (*OMS*, 137). This time he accepts without any real opposition the boy's insistence upon returning to his boat. He says no more about going far out alone. At this point, Santiago can say with impunity, about himself "he had attained humility . . . and he knew it was not disgraceful and it carried no loss of true pride" (*OMS*, 14). He has seen the tragic potential inherent in the Spaniard's isolated individualism; in his pride, which drove him beyond his true place in life, and with his deepened insight into its nature and destructive values, he has achieved the solidarity and love and peace for which the heroes of Ernest Hemingway have so mightily and futilely striven.[4]

The plight of the old man, Santiago, clearly parallels that of Hemingway's former Spanish-oriented heroes—but only to a certain point. Like the other Spanish-derived heroes, Santiago is not content to merely endure. He must show what a man can do, what can be accomplished in a violent and meaningless world where death conquers all. Salvation in such a life comes from acting courageously and thus affirming his worth as a man, from his faith in the value of individual excellence, and from his superior ability as a fisher-man. Even though the old man manages late in life to control his wildboar blood, his temperament has taken its toll by demanding that he demonstrate over and over again his defiant and individualistic spirit of *pundonor* and *particularismo*.

As in the case of Santiago, the *pundonor* of Hemingway's heroes after 1932 *(Death In The Afternoon)* drives them out past where they could go and still retain their physical and mental health, but here the parallel between Santiago and his counterparts breaks down, for Santiago is able to return. Whereas Santiago triumphs over the limitations of his nature in time and achieves a healthy balance between the forces of *particularismo* and humanism within himself, the other heroes do not.

Conclusion: Spoils of Spain

HEMINGWAY'S SUCCESSIVE visits to Spain in 1954, 1956, 1959, and 1960 showed that the author had not altered his attitudes about Spain or the Spanish people to any significant degree. His near hero worship of Antonio Ordóñez, a matador of great prowess, whose intense rivalry with Luis Miguel Dominguin he depicted in *The Dangerous Summer* (1960), revealed that this was still the way he wanted to be. In *The Dangerous Summer*, Hemingway re-emphasizes his affinity with the Spanish people in general and with the matador in particular. There is still the unmistakable longing for the supposed simpler, more elemental life of the Spanish world: "Finding the country unspoiled and being able to have it again. . . . I was as happy as I had ever been."

As for Antonio Ordóñez, he is foremost "a dominator" who kills with an "intelligent deadly anger." His performances are "deadly dangerous" because "he goes in just the way he should and takes all the chances." He has all the admired attributes of the matador: "Courage, skill in his profession and grace in the presence of danger of death." But what makes him most worthwhile to Hemingway is his "feeling of absolute superiority." "Antonio, I knew, was ruthless and had a strange implacable pride. . . . There were many things behind it and it had a dark side," Hemingway says. Elsewhere he remarks that Antonio "had the pride of the devil," and that he handled his bulls with "good form, arrogance and domination." In short, Antonio possesses all of the tendencies of *pundonor* and *particularismo* that characterize Hemingway's last four major protagonists.

This study has investigated the nature of the influence of certain aspects of Spanish thinking on Ernest Hemingway's treatment of character—especially that of his later heroes. I believe that a convincing case has been made for showing that Hemingway's association and identification with certain Spanish behavioral patterns and with the Spaniard's fatalistic world view led him to alter significantly his depiction of character from 1932 until the end of his career. It was in 1932—in the writing of *Death In The Afternoon*—that he defined his highest aspirations as man and artist in terms of Spanish attitudes toward life and death.

More specifically, whereas the earlier heroes—those least affected by the author's Spanish enthusiasms—evince a sense of vulnerability and helplessness in the face of life's uncertainties, his later heroes, as a result of Spanish tendencies, become distinctly aggressive and rebellious in nature. These later heroes bear a significant resemblance to the figures of Pedro Romero, Juan Belmonte, Manuel Garcia, and Manuel García Maera—Spaniards whom Hemingway apotheosized in previous works.

According to Philip Young and other prominent critics, Hemingway's early contacts with adversity—his inordinate exposure to death and violence—were evidently so shattering that he developed an exaggerated consciousness of the unending struggle of human existence. However, he found in the Spanish people not only his own tragic sense of the way things are, but also a fundamental attitude, characteristically gloomy, strongly individualistic, and at times anti-human, that seemed to satisfy the needs of his ailing psyche.

The core of this fundamental attitude is a sense of rebellion and a code of ethics both primitive and extreme in nature. Hemingway found that the Spaniard's temperament is such that he refuses to be classified within the general order of things: he refuses to be dominated in any way; he insists on being an exception and asserting his individual worth at every opportunity. The epitome of this spirit, which has come to be identified as the Spaniard's *particularismo,* was found to reside in the bullfighter. The matador, Hemingway found, is not content merely to endure in the face of life's hardships. His strange pride demands that he face danger and possible death over and over again to assert his individual skill and courage as a killer and as an artist through his particular art form. His self-imposed morality, which insists on strict adherence to a rigid and highly formalized set of rules for conduct, acts as a sort of secular religion based on the greatness of which the single man is capable when challenged by adversity.

Finally, Hemingway was particularly conscious of the dignity and the sense of glory the matador derives from killing quickly and in a way that gives emotional satisfaction. In describing the moment of the kill, Hemingway explains, "it should take place at such a time and in such a direct way as to give the most vivid spectacle of the authority of the human personality." Especially in the brief seconds of the last act of the bullfight the matador can demonstrate the greatest virtue. All events lead up to the actual encounter between the protagonist and death, when the matador and the bull are both ready for the kill. In the moment of the final sword thrust, what the Spanish call the moment of truth, the courage and discipline of the matador showed themselves clearest; with one stroke he can preserve both his honor and his dignity.

The value of dying well and the value of killing quickly and skillfully is the final expression of the matador's determination to show his contempt for death by meeting it head on. By imposing his will on death, Hemingway stresses, the matador is not in the hands of a whim-willed fate. But, as has been noted in tracing the Spanish element in the character of Hemingway's later heroes, at some point in the author's development he apparently began to have reservations about the morality of killing and about the ideal nature of the matador's anarchistic temperament in general. But by that time, he was so committed to the primitive and militant outlook of the matador that characterizes his later heroes that change was impossible. What resulted was the state of mental suffering—of perpetual conflict and moral confusion—observed in the minds of these last four protagonists. In trying to live out the reckless and rebellious lifestyle of the matador, they are led along a course of action that they later come to regret. The mind of the hero becomes a kind of psychic battleground in which two sets of attitudes struggle for authority. Which set wins out ultimately determines the fate of the hero.

Since Hemingway did choose ultimately to see the world through Spanish eyes, it is fitting now to say something about the depth and quality of the perspective this provided him. The first chapter revealed that Hemingway went to Spain with thoughts of death and decay haunting him; Philip Young marked the author as a

moribund individual deeply in need of some unifying and human-
izing force to mend his anguished soul. And Young felt that Spain
did, in fact, exert a positive influence on the writer. "Apparently
it did cure Hemingway," says Young, "by helping him overcome
the fright which seems once to have been nearly incapacitating."
Other critics agree that Hemingway's association with Spain, especially during the Spanish civil war, marked in his development
a happy turning point upwards from despair and self-centeredness
to a profound new respect for humanity and an unshakable faith
in the indomitability of man.

In one respect, certainly, Hemingway's identification with particular aspects of Spanish culture and with the Spaniard's fatalistic
world view contributed positively to his art. The image of the
matador and the symbolic purpose and structure of the bullfight
provided him with a thematic focus, a system of values, and even,
at times, a language with which to achieve his artistic goals. But
it seems to me inaccurate to conclude that the Spanish influence
on Hemingway was wholly good. The truth may, in fact, lie in
the other direction. That is to say, in accepting the sensibilities
and perceptions of the Spanish people, he also acquired the limitations of their point of view and range of expression. It was one
thing for the matador to seek meaning through moments of intensity
brought about through contact with death and violence. But for
the author, who desperately needed peace and harmony in his life,
to be constantly seeking out crisis situations was a matter of folly.
The author's commitment to the "now" bred self-absorption and
blinded him to the prospects inherent in past and future subjects.
Unamuno said that this commitment to *ahora* was the key to all
the Spaniard's problems—that he was a victim of the moment, and
hence had neither the time nor the disposition for an examination
of his own conscience. For a writer, such a deliberate attempt to
avoid looking and thinking about events and values outside his
immediate range of interests could only impoverish his creative
possibilities.

It is precisely this unwillingness to entertain any perspective other
than that dictated by *particularismo* and *pundonor* that underlies the

artistic weaknesses in the author's work from *The Green Hills Of Africa* until the end of his life. The critics that have been consulted on the nature of the Spanish character saw what Hemingway could not, or would not, grasp—that those elements of the Spaniard's nature the author chose to idealize, his *particularismo, pundonor,* and *casticismo,* were the destructive forces of a decadent spirit. These forces, which simply defined are the forces of extreme, anarchistic individualism and primitive aggression, were held by these critics to be the cause of the tragic disharmony that resulted in the disintegration of Spanish culture. Because Hemingway viewed these same forces with admiration and allowed them to dominate his thinking, he suffered a similar disintegration in both his person and in his art.

At times Hemingway did seem to question his beliefs—his point of view—what he thought he saw as the Spaniard's seemingly heroic attitude of resistance to authority and domination. Though he felt drawn to depict all that appeared simple and integral and noble in the person of the matador, he occasionally turned an eye toward what turned out to be complex, divided, and tragic. When he allows himself to acknowledge this contradiction—to treat the imperfections in his ideal heroes—he is immensely successful in creating convincing characters. For instance, at those moments when Robert Jordan and Santiago are compelled to look painfully at the flaws in their own natures, when the author attempts to understand the tragic source of the impulse to cruelty and death-dealing, true pathos is achieved.

Unfortunately, the rendering of psychological complexity was not Hemingway's forte; he was unable or unwilling to face and deal directly with the submerged aspects of his temperament that his Spanish enthusiasms forced to the surface. Too often in his later work, his desire to exalt Spanish values forces him to abandon psychic distance from his heroes and to concentrate primarily on surface aspects of character. In the case of Harry Morgan and Colonel Cantwell, the author is so intent in carrying out his masquerade as matador that the enactment of his "performance en route to death," with clenched teeth and sucked in belly, causes him to lose sight of the real subject—the mental confusion beneath the hero's protective covering. Control of the facade becomes so habitual in Morgan and Cantwell that it becomes one face, one attitude, for all occasions.

The moral excesses fostered by the posture of the matador are inseparable from the verbal excesses that show up as well in the later heroes. The extreme reticence of the earlier protagonists gives way to the venting of disconcerting hostilities and annoying prejudices that more and more intrude upon the objectivity of the writer's art. In particular, there is an unnerving impulse toward confessionism and exhibitionism—toward the melodramatic display of costume and ritual and toward sensationalistic shows of bravado. Correct bearing, bravery, honesty, integrity—the ingredients of *particularismo* and *pundonor*—become a personal attitude for the author that the heroes spend more time talking about than demonstrating, until, at times, the fiction becomes a parody of its former self.

Hemingway's consuming passion for bullfighting and his idealization of the matador appears to have been personally as well as artistically defeating. His defiant commitment to the matador's "eternal now" led him to take risks that eventually destroyed him through illness and disability. His pride as an artist allowed him to write only of what he had actually felt and seen; he believed that a man could only find meaning by immersing himself in experience and using his body as a testing ground for sensation. His Spanish sensibility told him that death and destruction, the great forces of *nada*, were not to be avoided anyway; hence, he cared little for the normal restraints imposed by a less fatalistic world view.

Like the matador, Hemingway was in rebellion against death, and his ability to transfer the bullfighter's values to his own art—to do work which demonstrated his individual greatness—was what made life tolerable and even enjoyable for him. He refused to be less than the champion; the spirit of compromise was anathema to him, for unlike his Santiago, he never really seems to have managed to attain humility. He had to assert his *particularismo* through action as a killer or as an artist—these were his terms. When it was clear to Hemingway that he would never write again, his friend A. E. Hotchner asked him why he could not rest on the work he had already done, and Hemingway replied: "A Champion cannot retire like anyone else. A champ should go out . . . like Antonio . . . on a particular good day." In trying to reason out what the forces had been that had crushed Hemingway, Hotchner noted: "He was a man of prowess and did not want to live without it: writing prowess, drinking and eating prowess. Perhaps when these powers diminished, his mind became programed to set up distorted defenses for himself. But if he could only be made to adjust to a life where these prowesses were not so all important. . . ." Hotchner might have recalled here what he had said to Hemingway at an earlier occasion: "Probably the moral is you never should have got mixed up with bullfighters."

Notes

Introduction

1. Carlos Baker, "Hemingway's Ancient Mariner" *Ernest Hemingway: Critiques of Four Major Novels,* ed. Carlos Baker (New York: Charles Scribner's Sons, 1962), p. 159.
2. *New York Journal-American,* July 3, 1961, p. 4.
3. Philip Young, *Ernest Hemingway: A Reconsideration* (University Park: The Penn State University Press, 1966), pp. 78, 79.
4. Arturo Baera, "Not Spain But Hemingway," *Hemingway And His Critics,* ed. Carlos Baker (New York: Hill & Wang, 1961), p. 203.
5. Jose Luis Castillo-Puche, *Hemingway Entre La Vida Y La Muerte* (Barcelona: Ediciones Destino, 1968), p. 18.
6. *Ibid.*
7. *Ibid.,* p. 14.
8. Jose Maria Iribarren, *Hemingway Y Los Sanfermines* (Pamplona: Editorial Gomez, S.L. Larrabide, 1970), p. 134.
9. *Ibid.,* 133.

Chapter 1

1. "Introduction: Citizen Of The World," *Hemingway And His Critics,* p. 5.
2. Carlos Baker, *Ernest Hemingway: A Life Story* (New York: Charles Scribner's Sons, 1969), p. 83.
3. *Ibid.,* p. 110.
4. *Ibid.*
5. *Ibid.,* p. 112.
6. *Ibid.*
7. Leo Lania, *Hemingway: A Pictorial Biography* (New York: The Viking Press, 1961), p. 43.
8. *Hemingway: A Life Story,* p. 158.
9. *Ibid.,* p. 129.
10. *Ibid.,* p. 141.
11. *Ibid.,* p. 129.
12. *Ibid.,* p. 130.
13. *Ibid.,* p. 147.
14. *Ibid.*
15. *Ibid.,* p. 154.
16. *Ibid.,* p. 149.
17. *Ibid.,* p. 144.
18. *Ibid.,* p. 209.
19. *Ibid.,* p. 204.
20. *Ibid.,* p. 203.
21. *Ibid.*
22. *Ibid.,* p. 224.

23. *Ibid.*, p. 243.
24. "Introduction: Citizen Of The World," *Hemingway And His Critics*, p. 6.
25. *Hemingway: A Life Story*, p. 264.
26. *Ibid.*, p. 246.
27. *Ibid.*
28. *Ibid.*, p. 316.
29. *Ibid.*, p. 313.
30. *Ibid.*, p. 325.
31. *Ibid.*, p. 313.
32. "Mechanized Doom: Ernest Hemingway And The American View Of The Spanish Civil War," *Critiques*, p. 98.
33. *Hemingway: A Life Story*, p. 301.
34. *Ibid.*, p. 302.
35. *Ibid.*, p. 353.
36. *Ibid.*, p. 316.
37. *Ibid.*, p. 336.
38. *Ibid.*, p. 446.
39. A. E. Hotchner, *Papa Hemingway* (New York: Random House, 1966), p. 236.
40. *Hemingway: A Life Story*, p. 481. Hemingway's appreciation of Goya was apparently engendered by a basic affinity of spirit as well as by an admiration of his talents as a painter. Paulino Posada has observed that, like Hemingway, "Goya was transformed into another man on bullfight days . . . he had a telluric and atavistic passion for bullfighting. . . . The painter from Fuendetodos admires danger and feels an itching for risk, which in our time is the emotion inspired by the work of Hemingway." Paulino Posada, 'Don Francisco The Painter of Bullfighting," *Los Torros: Bullfighting*, ed. Juan Fernandez Figueroa (Madrid: Indice, Artes Graficas, 1967), p. 78.
41. *Ibid.*, p. 513.
42. *Ibid.*, p. 392.
43. *Ibid.*, p. 407.
44. *Ibid.*, p. 301.
45. *Ibid.*, p. 511.
46. *Ibid.*, p. 512.
47. *Ibid.*, p. 535.
48. *Ibid.*, p. 546.
49. *Ibid.*, p. 512.
50. *Ibid.*
51. *Ibid.*, p. 546.
52. *Ibid.*, p. 549.
53. *Ibid.*, p. 553.
54. *Ibid.*, p. 546.
55. *Ibid.*, p. 544.
56. *Ibid.*, p. 552.
57. *Ibid.*, p. 333.
58. *Ibid.*, p. 380.
59. *Ibid.*, p. 514.
60. *Ibid.*, p. 550.

Chapter 2

1. Hemingway, *Playboy*, 10, no. 1, p. 124.
2. *Ernest Hemingway: A Reconsideration*, p. 63.
3. *Ibid.*, p. 55.
4. *Ibid.*, p. 40.
5. In *Death In The Afternoon* Hemingway is quite explicit about both the aesthetic and emotional satisfaction he derived from the bullfight; both, in fact, are inextricably bound together.
6. "Nightmare And Ritual In Hemingway," *Hemingway: A Collection Of Critical Essays.* ed. Robert P. Weeks (New Jersey: Prentice-Hall, 1962), p. 48.

Chapter 3

1. *Ernest Hemingway: A Reconsideration*, p. 60.
2. Carlos Baker, *Hemingway: The Writer As Artist* (New Jersey: Princeton University Press, 1951), p. 137.
3. "Nightmare And Ritual In Hemingway," *Hemingway: A Collection Of Critical Essays*, p. 42.
4. "Men Without Women," *Hemingway: A Collection Of Critical Essays*, p. 90.
5. Even though we are shown through Brett's influence on Romero that he too can be corrupted, his lapse is only temporary. Once Brett is out of the picture, he soon recovers his poise.
6. "The World Weighs A Writer's Influence," *Saturday Review* 44 (July 29, 1961), p. 18.
7. *Hemingway Entre La Vida Y La Muerte*, p. 236.
8. *Ibid.*, p. 206.
9. "The World Weighs A Writer's Influence," p. 18.
10. *Hemingway Entre La Vida Y La Muerte*, p. 206.
11. *Ibid.*, pp. 206, 207.
12. *Ibid.*, p. 207.

Chapter 4

1. This psychological aberration which allows Jake to excuse the uglier aspects of the fight in the name of art can be identified as a particularly Spanish habit of mind which becomes a permanent characteristic of the later heroes. Wearing the blinders induced by emotional sickness, Morgan, Jordan, Cantwell, and Santiago in a similarly questionable manner manage to justify the ritualistic inflicting of pain and death.
2. Max Eastman spoke of this ecstatic adulation with which Hemingway approached everything connected with the killing of bulls in the bullring. He concludes that "it is not death Hemingway writes about or travels to see, but killing." And he goes on to condemn the matador's theatrical pose as he torments and kills his bull, and his enthusiasm for killing—for courage, dominating, and blind cruelty. Eastman sums up Hemingway's morbid attraction to the bullring in these words: "We took this young man with his sensitive genius for experience, for living all the qualities of life and finding a balance among them—and with that too obvious

fear in him of proving inadequate—and we shoved him into our pit of slaughter, and told him to be courageous about killing. And we thought he would come out weeping and jittering. Well, he came out roaring for blood, shouting to the skies the joy of killing, the 'religious ecstasy' of killing—and most pathetic, most pitiable, killing as a protest against death."

3. Angel Ganivet, *Idearium Espanol* (Buenos Aires: Espasa-Calpe, 1945), p. 9. Translations from the works of Ganivet, Ortega y Gasset, and Miguel de Unamuno are the result of the combined efforts of Lawrence Broer and César Luis Rivera.

4. *Idearium Español*, p. 39.

5. Salvador de Madariaga, *Spain* (New York: Charles Scribner's Sons, 1930), p. 247.

6. *Idearium Español*, p. 44.

7. *Ibid.*, p. 63.

8. *Ibid.*

9. Jose Ortega y Gasset, *España Invertebrada* (Madrid: Revista de Occidente, 1951), p. 64.

10. *Ibid.*, p. 63.

11. *Ibid.*, p. ix.

12. *Ibid.*, p. 70.

13. E. Allison Peers, *Spain* (London: Methuen and Co., 1938), p. 7.

14. James Russell Lowell, *Impressions Of Spain* (New York: Houghton Mifflin, 1899), p. 39.

15. Miguel de Unamuno, *Mi Religión, y Otros Ensayos Breves* (Buenos Aires: Colección Austral, 1942), p. 33.

Chapter 5

1. About Hemingway's explicit identification with the matador, one recalls the author's remark to Morley Callaghan in *That Summer In Paris* after Hemingway had spat blood in Callaghan's face during a boxing episode: "That's what the bullfighters do when they're wounded. It's a way of showing contempt." Later, Hemingway identified the art of the bullfighter with his own so closely that in *The Dangerous Summer* he has his bullfighter companion fuse the two entirely. "There are days when you can't write at all," the matador says. "But they have paid to see you so you write as well as you can." "You've been writing all right lately," Hemingway answers. After more of the same, Hemingway concludes, "He was very pleased, always to call the faena writing." pt. 2, p. 66.

2. Hemingway's companion tells him, "We have very primitive emotions. . . . It's impossible not to be competitive."

3. This same fierce determination to be honest turns into self-conscious posturing on the part of Hemingway's later heroes—especially in the case of Harry Morgan and Colonel Cantwell.

4. It was in search of such knowledge that Hemingway suffered a fateful plane crash in 1958, which seems to have initiated a series of illnesses that beset him in the last years of his life.

5. Numerous friends of Hemingway's have commented on his complete intolerance of any writer who would not share his literary ideas and concepts. Whoever refused

to accept these without reservation was his bitter enemy. In later years a whole succession of friends incurred this treatment because they did not "measure up."

6. Hemingway's more recent depiction of Fitzgerald in *A Moveable Feast* was even more crushing.

7. "You Could Always Come Back," *Ernest Hemingway: The Man And His Work,* ed. John McCaffery (New York: The World Publishing Co., 1950), p. 140.

8. See page 61 in chapter four. This obsession with the glory of killing and dominating is focused in Hemingway's exclamation on page 33 of *Green Hills Of Africa:* "Isn't triumph marvellous?" [sic]

9. Miguel de Unamuno, *En Torno al Casticismo* (Buenos Aires: Espasa-Calpe, 1943), p. 18.

10. José Ferrater Mora, *Unamuno: A Philosophy Of Tragedy* (Berkeley: University of California Press, 1962), p. 8. Though some people might object to the idea of attributing such tendencies to the Spanish alone, it is significant that three such distinguished critics as Unamuno, Ganivet, and Gasset should have agreed so emphatically as to basic characteristics of the Spanish personality. And it was in the character of the matador that Hemingway seems to have found these forces operating so dramatically.

11. *Ibid.*

12. For further information on these two forces at work in Jake's nature, see "Hemingway's Don Quixote in Pamplona," by Robert Stephens, *College English* 23 (December, 1961), 216–218.

13. Castillo-Puche sees the bullfight as the very incarnation of Hemingway's own tortured spirit—cruel, and at the same time majestic, violent, and at the same time pacifying—reclothed in the beauty of art.

Chapter 6

1. Edgar Johnson, "Farewell The Separate Peace," *Ernest Hemingway: The Man And His Work,* ed. John McCaffery (New York: The World Publishing Co., 1950), p. 121.

2. Despite the hero's new aggressiveness, he is still depicted as a victim of outrageous fortune. And detectable beneath the stoical facade there still exists the tormented psyche of Nick Adams and Frederick Henry, suffering from profound feelings of persecution. Despite the spurious sense of chivalry behind Harry's unwillingness or inability to admit openly to suffering, he still suffers deeply the stings of suspected violent and unrelenting abuse. The suffering hero never really disappears completely beneath the endless shows of reckless courage and unreasoning bravado.

3. "Violence And Discipline," *Ernest Hemingway: The Man And His Work,* p. 244.

4. It is just because Harry's shows of asserting his masculinity are *conspicuous*—drawing so much attention to themselves and away from the narrative—that this is one of Hemingway's least successful novels. Harry expresses his manliness with calculated bravado. His conversation is reduced to a minimum, and his talk, as well as his actions, is largely a matter of pose and gesture. Harry is so persistent in asserting his fearlessness that this affected manly bluff soon wears on his own nerves as well as on the reader's.

5. It seems that Harry has achieved the dubious ability to ignore the more unpleasant aspects of violence that Jake was learning about in *The Sun Also Rises*. But it has resulted in a coarseness of spirit.

6. Jordan learns this new system from Pilar, the Spanish mother-confessor who constantly counsels him throughout his ordeal. He reflects: "She is a damned sight more civilized than you and she knows what time is all about. Yes, he said to himself, I think that we can admit that she has certain notions about the value of time. . . . Not time, not happiness, not fun, not children, not a house, not a bathroom, not a clean pair of pyjamas, not the morning paper. No, none of that. . . . So if you love this girl as much as you say you do, you had better love her very hard and make up in intensity what the relation will lack in duration and in continuity." This telescoping of time, in which duration is sacrificed for intensity and which Hemingway found most purely expressed in the last moment of the bullfight, becomes a supreme value for Harry Morgan and applies to the facing-death situations of all of Hemingway's later heroes.

7. Ironically, because of the author's desire to compensate for his earlier feelings of vulnerability, illustrated by Jake and Frederick Henry, he has now swung so far in the other direction that his present hero seems inhuman, both in the sense of being cruel and of being unreal as a fictional character. When the aggressive mask of the matador slips and the suffering, more complex character beneath is revealed, Hemingway is most engaging.

8. "Farewell The Separate Peace," *Ernest Hemingway: The Man And His Work*, p. 122.

9. *Ibid.*, p. 125.

10. "You Could Always Come Back," *Ernest Hemingway: The Man And His Work*, p. 163.

11. "A Portrait Of Mister Papa," *Ernest Hemingway: The Man And His Work*, p. 44.

12. Unamuno has noted that the Spaniard's strange combination of humanity and bestiality has contributed to a history of perpetual strife and discord—a duality of spirit, which the philosopher illustrated through the work *Don Quixote de la Mancha*. Unamuno says that the Spaniard's attempts to create a sense of unity, even motivated by the necessities of war, were from the start doomed to be betrayed by his more bestial self—by his anarchistic need for independence, his personal pride, and primitive aggressiveness. Critic Edwin Burgum observes that this same matter of temperament present in the mental processes of Hemingway's Spaniards creates a kind of tragic inevitability in Jordan's failure to realize his future goals of human solidarity. "Psychology Of The Lost Generation," *Ernest Hemingway: The Man And His Work*, p. 292.

13. "An American In Spain," *Ernest Hemingway: Critiques Of Four Major Novels*, p. 81.

14. Alvah Bessie observes in a review of *For Whom The Bell Tolls*, in *Critiques Of Four Major Novels*, edited by Carlos Baker, that Hemingway's unwillingness to come to grips with one of the major forces behind the defeat of the Spanish Republic—the Spaniard's refractoriness towards authority, his opposition to organization, which Ganivet pointed to as the most potent factor in his constitution—causes him to look for other scapegoats.

15. Hemingway had seen first hand and resented the results of Loyalist tactics of murdering non-participant citizenry, and, though he does not openly condemn his friends through Jordan, his disgust shows through in the description of the scene.

16. In an article entitled "The Spanish Tragedy," in *Critiques Of Four Major Novels*, Carlos Baker says that Hemingway was so saturated with the terminology and psychology of the bullfight that he could not help being drawn to its imagery in depicting the battle of other opposing forces. He observes that the entire massacre is organized in terms of the bullfight.

17. Here is another example of the hero's wearing of emotional blinders, the source of which can be traced to Jake Barnes' justification of violence and cruelty in the bullring.

18. "Nightmare And Ritual," *Hemingway: A Collection Of Critical Essays*, p. 49.

19. Once again is encountered the terror of the collective lust of "they" that turned on Frederick Henry to break his spirit. The fact that the threat of betrayal still remains a preoccupation of Hemingway's suggests that the author's early fear of disintegration is still a chief source of motivation beneath the stoical mask of these later heroes. Ironically, Hemingway now identifies the Spanish, themselves, whom he has come to rely on for protection against a world that kills and breaks, as part of that instrument that searches out the individual to taunt and destroy him. One cannot help asking, because of the extent of the author's depiction of entrapment and decline in a hostile world, whether this is not more revealing of an abnormal condition in the mind of the author than of the world he professes to describe.

Chapter 7

1. *Papa Hemingway*, p. 202.

2. "Hemingway's *Across The River And Into The Trees*," *Hemingway And His Critics*, p. 216.

3. Clinton S. Burhans, "*The Old Man And The Sea*: Hemingway's Tragic Vision Of Man," *Ernest Hemingway: Critiques Of Four Major Novels*, p. 152.

4. Clinton S. Burhans has written a brief but highly instructive article on the theme of solidarity and interdependence in *The Old Man And The Sea* entitled "Hemingway's Tragic Vision Of Man." He notes that two other striking examples of Santiago's opposition to the individualistic pull in his temperament are his constant references to baseball, which is far more a team sport than the individualistic bullfighting, his hero worship of Di Maggio, a noted team player, and his dreams of the young lions, who seem to symbolize love and humility as they cavort peacefully together.

Bibliography

Adams, Nicholson B. *España, Introducción a su Civilización*. New York: Henry Holt & Co., 1947.

Allen, John J. "The English Of Hemingway's Spaniards." *South Atlantic Bulletin* 27 (November 1961): 6-7.

Aronowitz, Alfred G., and Hamill, Peter. *Ernest Hemingway: The Life And Death Of A Man*. New York: Lancer Books, 1961.

Atkins, John. "Hemingway And The American Novel." *Wisdom* 3 (June 1958): 5-9.

_____. *The Art Of Ernest Hemingway: His Work And Personality*. London: Peter Neville, 1952.

Baera, Arturo. "Not Spain But Hemingway." In *Hemingway And His Critics*, edited by Carlos Baker, pp. 202-12. New York: Hill & Wang, 1961.

Baker, Carlos. *Hemingway: The Writer As Artist*. Princeton, N. J.: Princeton University Press, 1952.

_____. *Hemingway: A Life Story*. New York: Charles Scribner's Sons, 1969.

_____. *Hemingway And His Critics*. New York: Hill & Wang, 1961.

_____. *Ernest Hemingway: Critiques Of Four Major Novels*. New York: Charles Scribner's Sons, 1962.

_____. "Introduction: Citizen Of The World." In *Hemingway And His Critics*, edited by Carlos Baker, pp. 1-19. New York: Hill & Wang, 1961.

_____. "Hemingway's Ancient Mariner." In *Ernest Hemingway: Critiques Of Four Major Novels*, edited by Carlos Baker, pp. 156-74. New York: Charles Scribner's Sons, 1962.

_____. "The Spanish Tragedy." In *Ernest Hemingway: Critiques Of Four Major Novels*, edited by Carlos Baker, pp. 108-32. New York: Charles Scribner's Sons, 1962.

Barja, Cesar. *Libros Y Autores Contemporáneos*. Madrid: 1935.

Basave, Jr., Dr. Agustín. *Miguel de Unamuno y José Ortega y Gasset*. México: Editorial Jus, 1950.

Bell, Aubrey, F. G. *The Magic Of Spain*. New York: John Lane Co., 1912.

Bensusan, S. L. *Home Life In Spain*. New York: Macmillan Co., 1910.

Besore, John W. *Seneca, Moral Essays*, with an English Translation. New York: G. P. Putnam's Sons.

Betsky, Seymour. "A Last Visit." *Saturday Review* 44 (July 1961): 22.

Brenan, Gerald. *The Literature Of The Spanish People From Roman Times To The Present Day.* Cleveland: Meredian Books, 1957.

Burgum, Edwin Berry. "Ernest Hemingway And The Psychology Of The Lost Generation." In *Ernest Hemingway: The Man And His Work,* edited by John McCaffery, pp. 277-96. New York: World Publishing Co., 1950.

Burhans, Clinton S. *"The Old Man And The Sea:* Hemingway's Tragic Vision Of Man." In *Ernest Hemingway: Critiques Of Four Major Novels,* edited by Carlos Baker, pp. 150-55. New York: Charles Scribner's Sons, 1962.

Burz, John P. "Hemingway In Spain." *Contemporary Review* 195 (February, 1959): 103-105.

Callaghan, Morley. *That Summer In Paris.* New York: Coward-McCann, 1963.

Carpenter, Frederic I. "Hemingway Achieves The Fifth Dimension." In *Hemingway And His Critics,* edited by Carlos Baker, pp. 192-201. New York: Hill & Wang, 1961.

Castillo-Puche, Jose. *Hemingway Entre La Vida Y La Muerte.* Barcelona: Ediciones Destino, 1968.

Colvert, James B. "Ernest Hemingway's Morality In Action." *American Literature* 27 (November 1955): 372-85.

Cowley, Malcolm. "Nightmare And Ritual In Hemingway." In *Hemingway: A Collection Of Critical Essays,* edited by Robert P. Weeks, pp. 40-51. New Jersey: Prentice-Hall, 1962.

―――. "A Farewell To Spain." *New Republic* 73 (November 30, 1932): 76-77.

―――. "A Portrait Of Mr. Papa." *Life* 25 (January 10, 1949): 86-101.

D'Agostino, Nemi. "The Later Hemingway." In *Hemingway: A Collection Of Critical Essays,* edited by Robert P. Weeks, pp. 152-60. New Jersey: Prentice-Hall, 1962.

Downes, William Howe. *Spanish Ways And By-Ways.* Boston: Cupples, Upham & Company, 1883.

Eastman, Max. "Bull In The Afternoon." *New Republic* 75 (June 7, 1933): 94-97.

Ellis, Havelock. *The Soul Of Spain.* New York: Houghton Mifflin Co., 1915.

Espina, Antonio. *Ganivet, El Hombre y la Obra.* Buenos Aires: Espasa-Calpe, 1942.

Farrell, James. *"The Sun Also Rises:* A Commentary." In *Ernest Hemingway: Critiques Of Four Major Novels,* edited by Carlos Baker, pp. 4-6. New York: Charles Scribner's Sons, 1962.

Fennimore, Edward. "English And Spanish In *For Whom The Bell Tolls." ELH* 10 (March 1943): 73-86.

Fenton, Charles A. *The Apprenticeship Of Ernest Hemingway: The Early Years.* New York: Viking Press, 1958.

Fernández Almagro, Melchor. *Vida y Obra de Angel Ganivet.* Madrid: Revista de Occidente, 1953.

Fitzgerald, John D. *Rambles In Spain.* New York: Thomas Y. Crowell & Co., 1910.

Frank, Waldo. *Virgin Spain: The Drama Of A Great People.* Chile: Empresa Editora Zigzag, 1941.

Freedman, Richard. "Hemingway's Spanish Civil War Dispatches." *Texas Studies In Literature And Language* 1 (Summer 1959): 171-80.

Frohock, W. M. "Violence And Discipline." In *Ernest Hemingway: The Man And His Work*, edited by John McCaffery, pp. 235-61. New York: World Publishing Co., 1950.

Ganivet, Angel. *Idearium Español.* Buenos Aires: Espasa-Calpe, 1945.

Geismar, Maxwell. "Ernest Hemingway: You Could Always Come Back." In *Ernest Hemingway: The Man And His Work*, edited by John McCaffery, pp. 125-69. New York: World Publishing Co., 1950.

Guttman, Alan. "Mechanized Doom: Ernest Hemingway And The Spanish Civil War." *Massachusetts Review* 1 (May 1960): 541-61.

Hay, John. *Castilian Days.* New York: Houghton Mifflin Co., 1903.

Hemingway, Ernest. "A Man's Credo." *Playboy* 10 (January 1963): 120-124.

Hemingway, Leicester. *My Brother, Ernest Hemingway.* Connecticut: Faucett Publications, 1961.

Hicks, Granville. "The Shape Of A Career." *Saturday Review Of Literature* 45 (December 13, 1958): 16, 38.

_____. "A Feeling About Life." *Saturday Review* 44 (July 1961): 30, 38.

Hotchner, A. E. *Papa Hemingway.* New York: Random House, 1966.

Johnson, Edgar. "Farewell The Separate Peace." In *Ernest Hemingway: The Man And His Work*, edited by John McCaffery, pp. 113-24. New York: World Publishing Co., 1950.

Kashkeen, Ivan. "Alive In The Midst Of Death: Ernest Hemingway." In *Hemingway And His Critics*, edited by Carlos Baker, pp. 162-79. New York: Hill & Wang, 1961.

Kazin, Alfred. "Hemingway: Synopsis Of A Career." In *Hemingway: The Man And His Work*, edited by John McCaffery, pp. 170-83. New York: World Publishing Co., 1950.

Kerrigan, Anthony. "The Wandering Critic: Spain." *The Critic: A Catholic Review Of Books And The Arts* 20 (October-November 1961): 69-70.

Killinger, John. *Hemingway And The Dead Gods.* New York: Citadel Press, 1965.

Kinnamon, Kenneth. "Hemingway, The Corrida, And Spain." *Texas Studies In Literature And Language* 2 (Spring 1959): 44-61.

Lania, Leo. *Hemingway: A Pictorial Biography.* New York: Viking Press, 1961.

Levin, Harry. "Observations On The Style Of Ernest Hemingway." *Kenyon Review* 13 (Autumn 1951): 581-609.

Lowell, James Russell. *Impressions Of Spain.* New York: Houghton Mifflin Co., 1899.

Lyons, Leonard. "Trade Winds." *Saturday Review* 44 (July 1961): 8.

Madariaga, Salvador de. *Anarchy And Hierarchy.* New York: Macmillan Co., 1937.

_____. *Englishmen, Frenchmen And Spaniards.* London: Oxford University Press, 1929.

_____. *Spain: A Modern History.* New York: Frederick A. Praeger, 1958.

_____. "The World Weighs A Writer's Influence: Spain." *Saturday Review* 44 (July 29, 1961): 18.

Marra-Lopez, José R. "Hemingway: La Ultima Singuladura." *Insula* 16 (September 1961): 13, 16.

Marrero, Domingo. *El Centauro.* Puerto Rico, 1951.

Massip, José Maria. "A Hem tendremos que recordarlo conmovidos por lo que amó a España y a los españoles." *ABC,* July 4, 1961, p. 39.

MacLeish, Archibald. "His Mirror Was Danger." *Life* 51 (July 1961): 71.

McCaffery, John. *Ernest Hemingway: The Man And His Work.* Cleveland: World Publishing Company, 1950.

Miami Herald, July 3, 1961, p. 4.

Mora, José Ferrater. *Unamuno: A Philosophy Of Tragedy.* Berkeley: University of California Press, 1962.

New York Journal-American, July 3, 1961, p. 4.

New York Mirror, July 4, 1961, p. 3.

New York Times, July 3, 1961, p. 6.

Oldsey, Bernard S. "Hemingway's Old Men." *Modern Fiction Studies* 1 (August 1955): 32-35.

Opell, Horst. "Hemingway's *Across The River And Into The Trees.*" In *Hemingway And His Critics,* edited by Carlos Baker, pp. 213-26. New York: Hill & Wang, 1961.

Ortega y Gasset, José. *Obras.* Madrid: Espasa-Calpe, 1936.

_____. *España Invertebrada.* Madrid: Revista de Occidente, 1951.

_____. *Notas.* Buenos Aires: Espasa-Calpe, 1938.

Peers, E. Allison. *Spain.* London: Methuen & Co., 1938.

Perez, Gallego Candido. "Aportación española al estudio de Hemingway: Notas para una bibliografía." *Filología Moderna* 2 (October 1961): 51-71.

Pineyro and Peers. *The Romantics Of Spain.* Liverpool: Institute of Hispanic Studies, 1934.

Portunondo, José Antonio. "The Old Man And Society." *Americas* 4 (December 1952): 6-8.

Bibliography 127

Posada, Paulino. "Don Francisco The Painter of Bullfighting." In *Los Torros: Bullfighting*, edited by Juan Fernandez Figueroa, pp. 78–79. Madrid: Indice, Artes Graficas, 1967.

Sánchez Barbudo, Antonio. *Una Pregunta Sobre España*. México: Editorial Centauro, 1945.

Sanders, David. "Ernest Hemingway's Spanish Civil War Experiences." *American Quarterly* 12 (Summer 1960): 133-43.

Scott, Arthur L. "In Defense Of Robert Cohn." *College English* 18 (March 1957): 309-14.

Sentis, Carlos, "El último centauro de la generación perdida." *La Vanguardia Española*, July 4, 1961, p. 12.

Singer, Kurt. *Hemingway: Life And Death Of A Giant*. Los Angeles: Holloway House Publishing Co., 1961.

Spilka, Mark. "The Death Of Love In *The Sun Also Rises*." In *Hemingway And His Critics*, edited by Carlos Baker, pp. 80-92. New York: Hill & Wang, 1961.

Stein, Gertrude. "Hemingway In Paris." In *Ernest Hemingway: The Man And His Work*, edited by John McCaffery, pp. 17-25. New York: World Publishing Co., 1950.

Stephens, Robert O. "Hemingway's Don Quixote In Pamplona." *College English* 23 (December 1961): 216-18.

St. Petersburg Independent, July 3, 1961, p. 1.

"The Hero Of The Code." *Time* 77 (July 1961): 87-90.

Trilling, Lionel. "Hemingway And His Critics." In *Hemingway And His Critics*, edited by Carlos Baker, pp. 61-70. New York: Hill & Wang, 1961.

Unamuno, Miguel de. *En Torno al Casticismo*. Buenos Aires: Espasa-Calpe, 1943.

_____. *Mi Religión y Otros Ensayos Breves*. Buenos Aires: Espasa-Calpe, 1942.

_____. *Tragic Sense Of Life*. Translated by J.E.C. Flitch. New York: Dover, 1954.

Vasquez, José. "Hemingway: Bridge Between Two Worlds." *Americas* 13 (August 1961): 2-5.

Warren, Robert Penn. "Ernest Hemingway." In *Introduction To Modern Standard Authors Edition Of A Farewell To Arms*. New York: Charles Scribner's Sons, 1949.

Weeks, Robert. *Hemingway: A Collection Of Critical Essays*. New Jersey: Prentice-Hall, 1962.

Williams, Stanley T. *The Spanish Background Of American Literature*, 2 vols. New Haven: Yale University Press, 1955.

Young, Philip. *Ernest Hemingway: A Reconsideration*. University Park, Pa.: Pennsylvania State University Press, 1966.

Index